LEICESTER & RUTLAND
MURDER CASEBOOK

DAVID BELL

COUNTRYSIDE BOOKS

NEWBURY · BERKSHIRE

COUNTRYSIDE BOOKS
3 Catherine Road
Newbury, Berkshire

ISBN 1 85306 352 5

Designed by Mon Mohan

Produced through MRM Associates Ltd., Reading
Typeset by Acorn Bookwork, Salisbury, Wilts
Printed by J. W. Arrowsmith Ltd., Bristol.

For the five jays

Julie, Jane, Joanne, Jackie and Janette

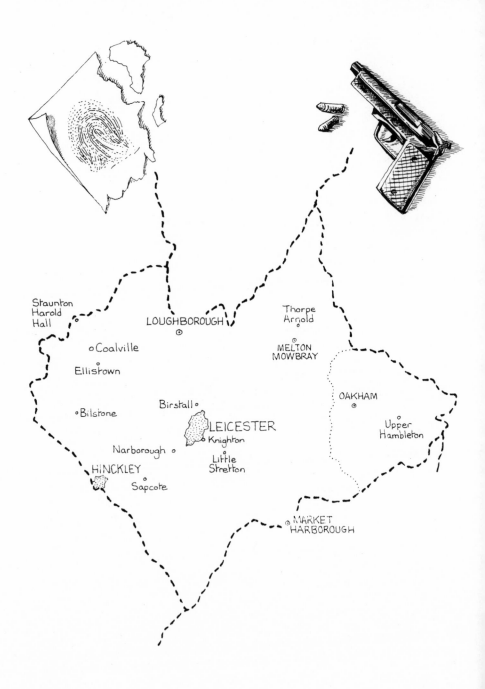

Contents

Acknowledgements

I would like to express my thanks to photographer John Bowker; the staff of the *Leicester Mercury* library; C Wendy East, author of *The Green Bicycle Murder*; Angela Atton and DI Mick Mills of the Leicestershire Constabulary HQ; Mrs Chris Mowle; the staff of the Leicestershire Record Office in Wigston; and Arthur Crane, author of *The Kirkland Papers*.

1

THE LEICESTERSHIRE CONSTABULARY

The present day Leicestershire Constabulary is the result of the combination of three police forces, and its current name dates from 1974.

In January 1828, the borough of Leicester resolved to set up its own police force and the Council Watch Committee decided to send to London for a copy of the rules of the Metropolitan Police to act as a model. They also decided that they should appoint an inspector of the Metropolitan force, Frederick Goodyer, as the superintendent of the new Leicester force, on an annual salary of £100. He took up his appointment in February 1828, with 50 constables under his command, each paid 18 shillings a week. The first police station was under the ancient Guildhall, which at that time was used as the town hall.

In 1839, Parliament passed the County Police Act, and Leicestershire became the sixth county to set up its own force. The county was looking for a first class man to lead the force, and offered a salary of £250 per annum. They were delighted that among the applicants was Frederick Goodyer of the Leicester Borough force. Despite their obvious disappointment at losing a fine chief, Leicester Borough supported his application and Frederick Goodyer became the first Chief Constable of Leicestershire in December 1839, serving in that position for 37 years. Gradually, the towns running their own separate police systems came under the County system: Market Harborough in 1847, Melton Mowbray and Hinckley in 1848, and Loughborough in 1858.

With the departure of Frederick Goodyer to head the county police in 1839, the Leicester Borough force appointed another Metropolitan officer, Robert Charters, as their own Chief Constable. This force, renamed the Leicester City Police when Leicester was granted city status in 1919, remained a separate body for 131 years.

In 1848, the neighbouring county of Rutland founded its own police force. Rutland was England's smallest county and the Rutland Constabulary was founded with a Chief Constable and one policeman! In 1951, the 23-strong Rutland force were amalgamated with that of their much larger neighbour to form the Leicestershire and Rutland Constabulary.

The final amalgamation took place in 1967, when the Leicester City Police came in to form a combined force. One final name change occurred in 1974 when the county of Rutland lost its fight to remain a separate county, and was incorporated into Leicestershire. The name of the police force once more became the Leicestershire Constabulary, as it had been when it began in 1839.

Following years of lobbying on behalf of women police officers by the county Federation of Women's Institutes and other organisations, Anne Hawkes became the county's first woman officer in 1944, though the city force were 15 years ahead, appointing their first WPC in 1929.

The Leicestershire Constabulary has had eight Chief Constables since 1839. Frederick Goodyer served from 1839 to 1876; Captain R V S Grimston from 1876 to 1889; Edward Holmes, OBE, KPM, from 1889 to 1928; Major C E Lynch-Blosse, KPM, from 1928 to 1949; John Taylor, CBE, QPM, DL, from 1950 to 1972; Alan Goodson, OBE, LLB, QPM, from 1972 to 1986; and Michael Hirst, BA, QPM, from 1986 to 1993. The current Chief Constable is Keith Povey, QPM, BA (Law) who was appointed in 1993.

The present Leicestershire Constabulary has 1,838 police officers, 746 civilians and 369 special constables, serving a population of 885,500.

2

ARISTOCRAT AND MURDERER

THE MURDER OF JOHN JOHNSON AT STAUNTON HAROLD, JANUARY 1760

L aurence Shirley, the 4th Earl Ferrers, was born in 1720 and inherited his title at the age of 25. He attended Oxford University but left without taking a degree. He owned large estates in Leicestershire, Derbyshire and Northamptonshire, and lived at Staunton Harold in north-west Leicestershire. He was said to be eccentric, but this seems to have been a euphemism for having a violent temper and for insisting on having his own way in every matter, large or small. His insane rages were not helped by his prodigious consumption of alcohol. He seems to have been thoroughly disliked by his fellow peers. His excommunication from the Church of England was a source of considerable embarrassment to his youngest brother, the Rev Walter Shirley!

Once, when guests he had summoned to dine with him at his home failed to attend, Earl Ferrers flew into a violent rage, horsewhipping and kicking his servants and throwing objects at everyone he saw. On a separate occasion, when some oysters delivered to Staunton Harold proved to be bad, he demanded that his servant swear that the carrier who had brought them from London had fraudulently exchanged them. When the servant was unable to comply with his master's demand, Ferrers stabbed him in the breast with a knife and beat him over the head with a candlestick.

Earl Ferrers' agent, Richard Clifford, had a handsome daughter named Margaret. She became Laurence Ferrers' mistress in 1743, and bore him four daughters between 1744 and 1749. Known as Mrs Clifford, Margaret became housekeeper at Staunton Harold

Maggie's Cottage – Johnson's home at Lount. (John Bowker)

Hall and kept that position even after his marriage. In 1752, Ferrers married Mary Meredith, the pretty 16 year old sister of Sir William Meredith of Henbury, Cheshire. Earl Ferrers was to claim later that Mary tricked him into marriage by ensuring that he was 'drunk at his betrothal, drunk at his wedding, and drunk for the whole period between the two.' As he was never of a sober disposition before or after he met his young bride, this ungallant claim seems a bit rich!

His treatment of his wife was so brutal – he often beat her, and frequently took a pistol to bed with him, threatening to shoot her before morning – that the Countess obtained a legal separation from him by Act of Parliament. This early form of divorce was not at all common, and the fact that Parliament granted it to the young Lady Ferrers provides an indication of the extent of Laurence Ferrers' brutal reputation.

The Act of Parliament made provision for an independent

12

income for the Countess from the rents of various farms belonging to the Ferrers estates. The Trustees of the scheme wished to appoint a trustworthy man to receive these rents and to ensure that the money was properly paid to Lady Ferrers. Their choice was Laurence Ferrers' steward, John Johnson, who was noted for his accuracy with accounts, his total honesty and his loyalty to the family. Johnson was nervous about taking the appointment, with good reason, given the erratic behaviour of his master. However, Earl Ferrers, who at this time had a high opinion of John Johnson, pressed his steward to accept the appointment. When Laurence Ferrers insisted, it was advisable to agree, and Johnson took the post.

It was not long before Johnson's fears were realised. Earl Ferrers began to say publicly that his steward was conspiring with the Trustees to rob him. In 1759, he tried to have Johnson evicted from his home, a farmhouse at Lount, but the Trustees intervened on his behalf. Ferrers became more and more incensed about the situation, and told his mistress Mrs Clifford that he would shoot the man. He even managed to delude himself that the sober, well-behaved Johnson was having a love affair with the Countess!

On Sunday 13th January 1760, Earl Ferrers called on John Johnson at his home. For once, he appeared to be in a friendly mood and even gave the steward a gift of some foreign coins. He told Johnson to come to Staunton Harold Hall at 3 pm on the following Friday to settle some outstanding accounts. On the Friday afternoon, Ferrers sent Mrs Clifford, her children, and all the male servants, away from the house. By the time John Johnson arrived, there were only three maidservants at the Hall: Elizabeth Saxon, Elizabeth Doleman and Elizabeth Burgeland. The latter admitted Johnson, who was punctual as usual. After keeping the steward waiting for ten minutes, Laurence Ferrers, sober for once, admitted him into his room and locked the door.

The three maids could hear the two men talking for about an hour. Then they heard their master shout, 'Sir, down on your other knee and declare what you have against Earl Ferrers!' This angry outburst was followed by the sound of a pistol shot. They went to the door of the room just as Laurence Ferrers was coming out. He told Elizabeth Doleman to go in and attend to Johnson who was inside with a gunshot wound in his side. She took the injured man upstairs and helped him to lie down on a bed. Suddenly Laurence Ferrers burst in, seized Johnson by his wig and said, 'I'll send a bullet through your head.'

Calming down again, Ferrers sent for Margaret Clifford and told her that he had shot Johnson. She expressed her distress at the action, but Ferrers told her that he had shot him justifiably, since Johnson would not confess to his guilt. Soon after this, Laurence Ferrers sent to Lount for Johnson's daughter, Sarah, though when she arrived he asked who she was. He sent Sarah up to see her father, then took her aside to say that he would provide for the family's needs if the steward died, provided they didn't prosecute. These swings between irrational rage and self-interested logic were typical of Earl Ferrers' behaviour. It was not long before he was back at Johnson's bedside swearing and abusing him.

Johnson asked Earl Ferrers to send to Ashby-de-la-Zouch for the surgeon Dr Kirkland, and a boy on a horse was dispatched.

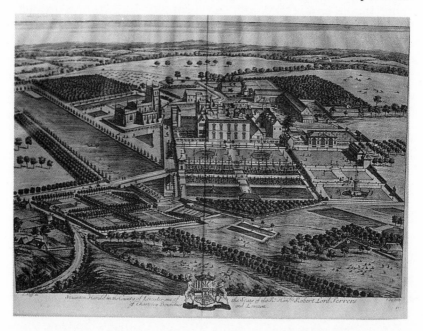

Staunton Harold Hall in the 18th century. (John Bowker/Newlands House Cheshire Home)

14

Staunton Harold Hall today. (David Bell)

The lad, Henry Wales, arrived at the doctor's house in Ashby at 5 pm; the doctor was out at the village of Coleorton, and a servant rode over to give him the message that John Johnson was near to death at Staunton Harold Hall. On his way to Staunton Harold, the cautious Dr Kirkland called at Johnson's house at Lount, to find out more about what had occurred. When he learned that Johnson had been shot by Earl Ferrers, Dr Kirkland went to the Hall on foot. He took several burly coalminers with him in case it was necessary to arrest Earl Ferrers, but on the way they were met by Elizabeth Saxon. She was in great distress, and told the surgeon that Ferrers was loading all his guns and threatening to shoot anyone who attempted to arrest him.

Dr Kirkland sent his companions back and went on to the Hall alone. In the yard, he met Mrs Clifford and an inebriated Earl Ferrers. After making sure that the doctor had come alone, Ferrers took him affably by the arm and accompanied him into the house. As they walked, he told Kirkland that he had shot Johnson, and had done it deliberately, but since the man was not dead the doctor had better do what he could for him. He then added ominously that if the man died, he would shoot anyone who tried to arrest him.

15

Dr Kirkland examined John Johnson and found that he had been shot in the left side, just below the bottom rib. The bullet was still inside him, and causing him great pain in the bowel. As the surgeon attempted to work out the path of the bullet, Ferrers happily demonstrated the angle of the revolver at the time of the shooting. This was somewhat callous, as both the injured man and his daughter were listening to every word. Ferrers was amazed that the ball was still inside the victim, and wondered aloud how it was that a bullet that had passed clean through a wooden board while he was practising would not go through a man.

Although Dr Kirkland could see that John Johnson was fatally wounded, and that nothing could be done for him, he took the highly sensible decision to lie about it. He reassured the volatile peer that his victim would make a full recovery. Ferrers insisted that the doctor should stay the night and sent for a supper of cold turkey and brawn. Dr Kirkland had no appetite; Laurence Ferrers did not eat much either but he continued to drink long into the night. During a long rambling conversation, Ferrers told the surgeon that he had tried to force Johnson to sign a paper admitting that he had been cheating and plotting against him ever since being made receiver of the rents. When Johnson had protested that he had never done anything against Laurence Ferrers' best interests, the earl had told him to kneel and beg his forgiveness. The man had gone down onto only one knee. This had been insulting, so Ferrers had ordered him onto both knees, then told him he was about to die and shot him with a horse pistol.

From time to time, Dr Kirkland went out to attend to his patient. Each time he returned, he told the inebriated peer that he thought the man would get better. When Earl Ferrers reeled off all his grievances against John Johnson, the doctor used enough discretion to agree that the earl had been much provoked. Throughout his long monologue, Laurence Ferrers reiterated that the shooting of the steward was not a hasty action, but was premeditated and deserved. At one stage he threatened, 'If he recovers, I will make him confess his being a rogue to me, or I will shoot him through the head or heart. Be sure Kirkland, you don't tell me any lies, for by God, I shall break your head if you do.'

Margaret Clifford came in at one point and asked if Johnson

would not be better taken home. Ferrers would have none of it, insisting that the injured man remain at the Hall. Later Ferrers got even more drunk, boasting to Dr Kirkland about his sexual conquests. He went to the room where John Johnson was lying, and began mocking him and abusing him. He worked himself up into a towering rage, pulled the bedclothes off and made as if to strike him. Sarah Johnson lay across her father's body to protect him, and Dr Kirkland and Mrs Clifford somehow managed to get Earl Ferrers to go to his own room.

As soon as he was alone with his daughter and Dr Kirkland, John Johnson begged them to get him away from Staunton Harold Hall. The doctor thought that this might be wise. If Laurence found out that the man was dying, he would realise that he had been deceived, and would again fly into a violent rage. He arranged with Sarah Johnson for her to signal by putting a lighted candle in the window, then left. Later he returned with eight men and they loaded John into a chaise. This they carried on poles, taking him to his own home in Lount. He died in his own bed at 9 am the next day.

A large crowd of colliers gathered outside Staunton Harold Hall the next day, intending to seize Earl Ferrers. They allowed Mrs Clifford and her children to leave unharmed. When Laurence Ferrers saw the men, he invited them to come in for food and drink, but they would have none of it. Told that Johnson was dead, he did not believe it at first, but then said that the man was a scoundrel and a villain, declaring, 'I glory in his death.' Although he was waving a pistol, two of the men seized Ferrers and he was taken to Ashby-de-la-Zouch. There he was lodged at the White Hart public house until the next day when the coroner's inquest brought in a verdict of wilful murder.

Earl Ferrers was taken first to Leicester county gaol, but as a peer of the realm he could not be tried at the assizes. On 11th February, he was transported in his own carriage to London and remanded to the custody of Black Rod, to await trial by the House of Lords. He was lodged in the Round Tower of the Tower of London, where he remained for two months. Two wardens were constantly in the room with him, and another outside the door. Two guards with fixed bayonets were posted at the bottom of the stairs and a third on the drawbridge. For once in his life, Earl Ferrers drank moderately, taking a spoonful of brandy with his breakfast, a pint of wine with his dinner and a further pint with his supper.

While in the Tower, Ferrers executed deeds leaving £6,000 to his four natural daughters, payable when they reached 21, or on earlier marriage. He also left £1,200 to the children of John Johnson, the murder victim!

On 16th April 1760, the trial before the House of Lords began in Westminster Hall. Lord Henley, Keeper of the Great Seal, who had been created Lord High Steward for the occasion, acted as judge. The prosecution was led by Sir Charles Pratt, the Attorney General, and Sir Charles Yorke, the Solicitor General. The prosecution witnesses were Dr Kirkland, Sarah Johnson, and the three maidservants who were present at Staunton Harold at the time of the murder. Each gave evidence of what they had seen and heard on the afternoon and evening of Friday 18th January. Mrs Clifford was not called, due to the unofficial nature of her relationship with the accused.

Had the charge been a lesser one than murder, Earl Ferrers would have been represented by counsel but this was not permitted in a capital offence. Since he had been persuaded by his family to plead not guilty due to insanity, he had to be astute and rational enough to conduct his own defence, while at the same time trying to convince the House of Lords that he was mad!

He had little difficulty in persuading family members to say that they regarded him as a lunatic, and several servants confirmed that he was 'cracked in the head'. One piece of evidence produced in support of this was given by a Peter Williams who had been looking after Earl Ferrers' mare. Ferrers had been dissatisfied, and when he collected the animal he had knocked down the man's wife, then run Williams through with a sword causing a serious wound. The reply of Sir Charles Yorke, the Solicitor General, is fascinating: he commented that this kind of action was an everyday occurrence and entirely justified when a servant was negligent. He dismissed the evidence saying that if this was a symptom of madness, then few people would be sane.

Earl Ferrers was not allowed, under the law of the land, to give his evidence under oath. Although he could make an unsworn statement, he could not be questioned by the prosecution. This meant that his words were given less weight. However, he spoke clearly and well, claiming that his conscience did not

18

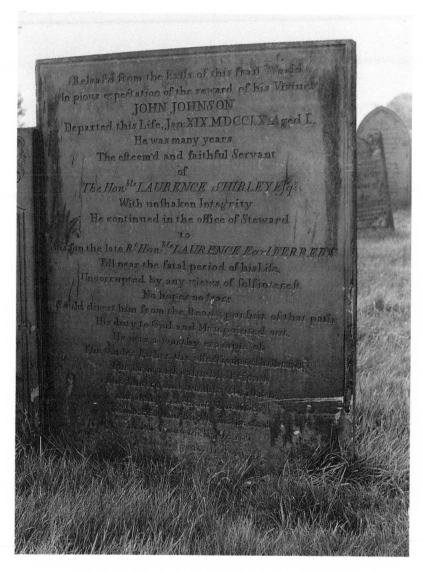

Johnson's gravestone in Breedon-on-the-Hill churchyard. (John Bowker)

condemn him for the crime because he had no preconceived malice. The action was done in haste and fury, and was the result of a disordered imagination.

The case put by Sir Charles Yorke was that Laurence Ferrers had acted deliberately and knew the consequence of what he was doing. He pointed out that Ferrers had told Sarah Johnson that he would maintain her family if they did not prosecute. His final telling cut was that the peers only had to look at the way Ferrers had presented his case 'with sense and sagacity' to conclude that he was indeed sane.

The House of Lords unanimously found Laurence Ferrers guilty of murder, and he was sentenced to death. He thanked the House for a fair trial, and apologised for his insanity defence, saying that it had been prevailed on him by his family. He referred to the murder as a 'fatal accident', and again denied any malice. The Lord High Steward pronounced the death sentence, condemning Earl Ferrers to be hanged at Tyburn (where Marble Arch now stands) on 21st April.

However, the execution was postponed until the 5th May. Earl Ferrers petitioned the king, George II, asking that he be beheaded as befitted his rank but received no reply. To the very end, he regarded it as unfitting that a nobleman should die on the scaffold like a common felon. Mrs Clifford moved to London with her four daughters, and took lodgings in Tower Street. Although she went to the Tower three times, she was not allowed to enter, though the children were permitted to visit their father regularly. Earl Ferrers and Mrs Clifford were allowed to correspond in writing, and exchanged letters daily.

No one could remember a peer being hanged before in England, and thousands were determined that they would come and watch the historic event. Because of the crowd, the procession from the Tower to the place of execution took two and three-quarter hours. Earl Ferrers insisted on making the journey in his own landau-and-six, rather than the coach provided. Accompanying him in his carriage were Sheriff Vallaint and the Chaplain of the Tower. Grenadier Guards led the procession, followed by a carriage, then Earl Ferrers' landau, then two mourning coaches, the horse-drawn hearse and a further contingent of Grenadiers.

As Earl Ferrers ascended the scaffold, the immense crowd saw that he was wearing a magnificent white suit, embroidered with silver. In fact, he had insisted on wearing his wedding suit, on the grounds that it had been his marriage that had led him to the gallows. He conducted himself with great composure, though the dignity of the occasion was marred when a fight broke out between the hangman and his assistant over the five guineas which the condemned peer had handed to the wrong man. This 'tip' was to ensure that his death was a quick one. Unfortunately the drop at that time was only 18 inches, insufficient to break the condemned man's neck, and it was necessary to tip the hangman to go under the platform and swing on the hanged man's legs to swiften his strangulation.

The signal for the execution was given by Sheriff Vallaint, Ferrers himself refusing to give it. The death on this occasion, given a little help from beneath the platform, was relatively quick, Earl Ferrers taking about four minutes to die. The persistent story that Ferrers was hanged on a silken rope is impossible to verify, and must remain an often-quoted legend.

An hour after the execution, Laurence Ferrers' corpse was taken down, placed into a coffin and transported to Surgeon's Hall. There, as laid down in the sentence, it was 'anatomised'. This meant that the entrails were removed from the abdomen, and that incisions were made across the throat and down the chest. The mutilated body was then placed in an upright open coffin, and put on public display for five days, guarded by an armed soldier. On 10th May, the body was buried in St Pancras' church.

The trial and execution of Laurence, Earl Ferrers has an important niche in history. In his scholarly book *The Kirkland Papers*, Arthur Crane argues that the Ferrers trial played some part in ensuring that England did not have a French-style revolution. The fact that an aristocrat could be tried and hanged for killing a servant might have persuaded many that the English law was applicable to all.

The Ferrers title passed first to Laurence's brother Washington, then to his second brother Robert. The present Earl Ferrers, a government spokesman in the House of Lords, is descended from the youngest of the brothers, the Rev Walter Shirley.

It was soon after Robert had inherited the title that he was able to fulfil Laurence's wish for his body to be brought back to

Leicestershire. Twenty-two years after the execution, the body of the hanged peer was re-interred in the family vault at Staunton Harold. About two miles away, the remains of John Johnson lie in a much humbler grave in the churchyard at Breedon-on-the-Hill. Even in death, rank continues to play its part.

3

FOUR 19th CENTURY MURDERS

THE MURDER OF MRS MASSEY AT BILSTONE, 1800; OF JOHN PAAS
AT LEICESTER, 1832; OF EDWARD AND JAMES WOODCOCK AT
THORPE ARNOLD, 1856; AND OF JOSEPH TUGBY
AT COALVILLE, 1877

Death by hanging was the usual penalty for murder in the 19th century, but it is interesting to note that of all the people hanged in Leicestershire, less than half were murderers! Others were given the ultimate penalty for forgery, burglary, horse-stealing and rick burning. The latter was regarded not only as a crime against the individual land-owner, but also as a political offence against the natural order of things. Arson with a hint of treason, no less.

A similar 'revolutionary' crime was the breaking of knitting frames. The death penalty for this was abolished in 1814 but reintroduced in 1817. It was of particular interest in Leicestershire, because those who broke the knitting frames were called Luddites after 'Ned Lud' of Anstey. On one day, 17th April 1817, six men were hanged in Infirmary Square, Leicester, for the crime of being Luddites, together with another man hanged for rick burning.

These men were hanged to deter others from taking the same path, though whether hanging has ever been a deterrent is very debatable. When public hanging for robbery was still carried out, the thousands who turned out to watch were frequently robbed of their purses and handkerchiefs. The pickpockets regarded a public hanging as one of their most rewarding working days.

However, it is with the crime of murder that we are most concerned, and the following four murders from the 19th century are of particular historical interest.

* * *

John Massey was a thickset man who earned the nickname 'Topsy-Turvey' through his skill as a wrestler. His claim was that he could throw to the ground any man in four counties. Massey lived in the Leicestershire village of Bilstone close to the point where the four counties – Leicestershire, Derbyshire, Staffordshire and Warwickshire – meet. A hedger and ditcher by trade, he had a reputation of being a hard, bad-tempered man, and definitely not a man to cross. His drinking companions treated him with respect due more to fear than friendship.

He had driven his first wife to an early grave through a mixture of ill treatment and neglect, and then married again. In 1800, he fatally injured his second wife by beating and kicking her, then threw her into the Bilstone mill-race to drown. When his ten year old stepdaughter tried to intervene, he threw her into the water too. However, she survived to become the main witness at his trial for murder at the Leicester Assizes.

Found guilty and sentenced to be hanged, this brutal man requested that he should be buried between his two wives. Perhaps he thought they might be missing his company! Probably his main reason was to avoid his body being turned over to the medical profession for dissection. However, his body was neither dissected nor buried.

After his execution at Red Hill, Birstall, in 1801, the judge ordered his body to be taken back to Bilstone for gibbeting. The gibbet should not be confused with the gallows. Men were hanged on the gallows, but their bodies were then sometimes hung in a cage of metal bands, on a gibbet, close to the scene of their crime. John Massey's corpse hung in chains near Bilstone for over 18 years, long after the flesh had rotted from his bones! The theory behind the gibbeting of criminals was that it would act as a deterrent to others, putting the fear of God into them. How effective this proved is doubtful; Topsy-Turvey's old drinking cronies used to stagger up from the public house to pay their respects to his corpse, toasting his 'health' and even pouring ale into what was left of his mouth. Eventually, Massey's skull was stolen from the gibbet by 19th century vandals in search of a grisly souvenir.

24

The gibbet post at Bilstone, where the body of John Massey hung for 18 years. (David Bell)

The post on which he was gibbeted can still be seen by the side of the road from Bilstone to Congerston. It (usually) bears a notice that reads: 'This gibbet was erected here ¼ of a mile from the scene of a murder committed by John Massey February 1800'. However, the sign has to be replaced at regular intervals as it is frequently stolen by 20th century vandals in search of an unusual souvenir. It seems that people's behaviour does not really change!

*   *   *

The survival of this gibbet post often leads to the claim that John Massey was the last man to be gibbeted in Leicestershire, but this is incorrect. That dubious honour belongs to James Cook of Leicester. He lived in Wheat Street but he had a book-binding business on Wellington Street. In 1832 he was being pressed for payment of a debt of twelve shillings by an engraver and tool cutter named John Paas. When Paas came up from London to collect the debt in person, he called on Cook at his business premises. The 21 year old bookbinder decided to avoid paying his bill by beating Paas to death with an iron bar.

He then set about the gruesome task of disposing of the dead man. First he dismembered his body with a saw and a meat cleaver, fortifying himself with alcohol during this messy task. Next he lit a fire in his open grate and began to burn the flesh of his victim. This took him the best part of a day, and as he drank continually, he ended the day in a very drunken state. Throwing the last part of the body onto the fire, he locked up, then weaved his way unsteadily back to his house.

During the night, the chimney at the premises in Wellington Street caught fire and neighbours had to break in. On the open fire they found a huge piece of 'meat' blazing away. They fetched James Cook to the scene, and he explained that he was burning some meat he had bought for his dog but had then found to be rotten. His neighbours were unsatisfied but allowed Cook to go. He did not go home however; realising that he would be found out, he made a run for it. He walked ten miles north to Loughborough, and from there he caught a stage coach heading for Manchester.

The next day, in Leicester, surgeons examined the meat and found that it was a human thigh bone and pelvis. On the Wellington Street premises, the police discovered the bloodstained clothing and a leather pencil case belonging to John Paas. A reward was put up for Cook's capture, and two police officers set out in his pursuit. They caught up with him as he was being rowed out from Liverpool docks to a ship bound for America. He tried to swim ashore but was soon taken and brought back to Leicester to stand trial.

James Cook confessed his crime, and his trial before Baron Vaughan on 8th August was a mere formality. He was hanged two days later outside the Welford Road gaol, watched by a crowd of 30,000 onlookers. His body was gibbeted at the junction of Aylestone Road and Saffron Lane, and a further 20,000 people came to see his displayed body. The people who came to gawk were so riotous and licentious in their behaviour that the authorities realised that this was no deterrent. After only three days his body was taken down and buried on the spot. The origi-

Gibbet irons – last used on the body of James Cook in 1832. Cook was the last man to be gibbeted in Leicestershire. (Leicestershire Museums, Arts and Records Service)

nal gibbet irons used on James Cook were displayed at the Guildhall, near Leicester Cathedral, for many years, but in December 1994 they were moved to the National Prison Museum near Rugby, and a replica set is now displayed at the Guildhall.

* * *

William Brown was born in Scalford, near Melton Mowbray, in 1823, and he had two nicknames. The one he preferred was 'Peppermint Billy', which referred to his father's occupation of making mints. His other name, 'Blinking Billy', came about through an eye affliction that caused him to blink continuously.

Billy got into bad company, and in 1843 he was sentenced to ten years' transportation for stealing from a house at Newton Linford. He served his sentence in Tasmania, returning to England in 1856. On the sea voyage back, he told a member of the ship's crew that he intended to have his revenge on the person who had caused his transportation, boasting that he would murder him.

On 20th June, baker Alfred Routen set out in the early hours of the morning to travel from Asfordby to Grantham. He passed through Melton Mowbray, and came to the tollgate at Thorpe Arnold. He called out but the 70 year old gatekeeper did not appear, so the baker opened the door of the gatehouse and went in. There he found the gatekeeper, Edward Woodcock, lying dead. Beside him lay the body of his ten year old grandson, James.

The police were sent for, and they found that the gatekeeper had been stabbed many times and shot through the chest. The young boy had had his throat cut. Even the case-hardened police officers were in distress at the brutality of the scene. The Chief Constable of the county, Frederick Goodyer, arrived to take charge. Among the clues he found were a tobacco stopper and a large pistol of a type used by Australian bushrangers. It was quickly decided that the killer had left them behind.

Two further witnesses came forward. Joe Burbridge reported how a man had asked him whether Edward Woodcock lived alone in the gatehouse. A lad called Henry Read said that two days earlier a man had grumbled to him that the gatekeeper had refused him a drink of water. Both witnesses described a tall thin man who blinked all the time. The police immediately thought of 'Peppermint Billy' Brown, born only three miles away. The hunt was on.

A reward of £20 was put up, and William Brown's description circulated throughout Leicestershire and other counties. Four days later, news came from Yorkshire that a man answering Peppermint Billy's description had been arrested. He had walked into a public house in Weatherby, just as the publican was reading a description of the wanted man in his local paper, the *Leeds Mercury*.

Billy was brought back to Melton Mowbray by train, and appeared before the magistrates. He was committed for trial at the next assizes. The discovery of his bloodstained clothing close to the Thorpe Arnold tollgate was the final piece of evidence that sealed his fate. The motive for the murders was never settled, as Peppermint Billy denied his guilt to the end, but it is thought to have been either revenge against Edward Woodcock or theft. Young James Woodcock died simply because he was staying with his grandfather at the time.

Peppermint Billy was hanged outside the gates of Welford Road prison before a crowd of 25,000, at Leicestershire's very last public execution. At his death, his father made the laconic and seemingly callous comment: 'Well done, Billy. Yer've died a brick.'

* * *

Joseph Tugby was a 65 year old pedlar from County Durham, who came to Coalville in August 1877 to sell wares to the miners. He spent the last evening of his life drinking in The Stamford and Warrington Arms on Coalville's High Street. He joined in the pub singing with three local drinkers, James Satchwell, John Upton and John Swift. From time to time, the pedlar peered into an empty biscuit tin, a tantalising action designed to make his companions extremely curious.

When Joseph left the pub, he walked up Station Street (now called Hotel Street) to the footbridge over the railway line, unaware that he was being followed by his three fellow drinkers. On the footbridge the three men caught up with him and an argument began. Soon Joseph Tugby was receiving a savage beating and kicking.

The fatally injured pedlar was found just after midnight by two miners, his empty biscuit tin beside him. Constable Hardy was sent for, and Joseph Tugby was loaded into a wheelbarrow and carted back to the pub, then on to the Ashby Union. Writing up his notebook later, PC Hardy expressed himself tersely: 'Aug 31st. Found Tugby laying at the bottom of the steps of the foot railway bridge, all over bruises. Took him to the Union. He died at 10 am the next day.'

Two of the attackers, James Satchwell and John Upton, had left the scene of the attack to go to the Royal Oak, where a Charles Clifton overheard them talking about the affray. The police were sent for, and James Satchwell made a statement that the deed had been done by the absent member of the trio, John Swift. He said that 19 year old Swift had asked his two companions to 'keep garrison' (ie keep watch) while he 'sorted out' Tugby. When passers-by were heard, Swift had become agitated and kicked the old pedlar down the steps of the footbridge. Satchwell and Upton were arrested for wilful murder, and a search was started for the missing John Swift.

On 4th September, the police received a letter from a local wheelwright and evangelist, Richard Page, which said that he thought that Swift was hiding in his parents' cottage in Grange Road, Hugglescote. PC Hardy went to the cottage, with Inspector Clarke and Inspector Brewill. In the bedroom they spotted a trapdoor in the ceiling. Using a ladder to gain access, they entered the attic and found John Swift lying on a bed.

Swift was arrested, and when he heard what James Satchwell had told the police, he gave them a different story. In this version, Satchwell had started the fight with the Durham pedlar and had thrown him off the bridge.

At the trial of the three men in November, the two versions of the events were given, but the jury could not decide which was true. All three were found guilty, but a recommendation for mercy was added. This was ignored by the judge and the three men were sentenced to be hanged. Their execution on 27th November was a noteworthy one. It was the first hanging to take place inside Leicester county gaol on Welford Road, and for the first time, no newspaper representatives were present. This infuriated the *Leicester Journal* who called it a 'secret execution'.

Before he died, John Swift confessed that he alone had committed the murder. With astounding generosity of spirit, James Satchwell and John Upton forgave their young friend for the lies which had incriminated them! Despite Swift's last minute confession all three men were hanged together. It was Leicestershire's last triple hanging.

4

AN OFFICER AND A GENTLEMAN

THE MURDER OF BELLA WRIGHT NEAR LITTLE STRETTON,
JULY 1919

Annie Bella Wright, always known by her middle name, lived
with her parents in the village of Stoughton about three
miles east of Leicester, though she was born and went to school
in Somerby about twelve miles away. She left school at the age of
13, working first in domestic service in Tugby, then as a shop
assistant in Leicester. She returned to domestic service but like so
many women during the First World War, Bella found that there
were better paid jobs in factories, the male employees having
been called up to fight for their country.

By 1919, she was working as a factory hand making pneumatic
tyres at Bates' Rubber Mill in Leicester. One of her workmates
was Sally Ward. Bella struck up a friendship with Sally's brother,
Archie, who was serving as a stoker in the Navy. Although they
were not officially engaged, and Archie was four years younger
than Bella, it was generally accepted that they were courting and
that their friendship would progress further after Archie was
demobbed.

Bella could buy tyres cheaply from her employers, and she
became quite a keen cyclist, although she only cycled locally.
When she set out on her bicycle on the evening of Saturday 5th
July 1919, her 22nd birthday was only nine days away. The
notion that she would not reach her next birthday never entered
her head. She cycled from Stoughton to Evington to post three
letters, including one to Archie Ward. In Evington, she met Kathleen Power delivering the evening post, and she handed the letters
over to her, saving herself the trouble of going to the post office.

She rode home to Stoughton, then went on three miles to Gaulby to visit the home of her uncle, George Measures, a well known local character with a bushy beard and a wooden peg leg. Despite having a little trouble with her bike chain, and meeting another cyclist on the way, she had time to pick an armful of gorse to give to her aunt. She arrived at George's house at a quarter past seven, and was delighted to find that her cousin Margaret was down from Yorkshire, together with her new baby and her husband James. Bella stayed at the cottage in Gaulby for over one and a half hours, talking to her relations and cuddling the new baby. She found that James, a miner, was very interested in bicycles and she told him about the tyre factory where she worked. She did not set off to cycle back to Stoughton until almost nine o'clock.

On the ride home something dreadful must have occurred, because at 9.20 pm Bella's body was discovered by a passing farmer, Joseph Cowell, as he was walking along the old Roman road known officially as Gartree Road, but always referred to locally as the Via Devana. Bella was lying half on the road, half on the verge, and had bled profusely from the nose or mouth; there was a considerable pool of blood around her head. Her cycle was lying on the road, close by; it appeared that she had met with a tragic road accident. As Mr Cowell lifted Bella onto the grass, he realised that although she was still warm, she was actually dead. He moved her bicycle off the road, leaning it against a field gate, then returned to his farm. Once there he sent two farmworkers to guard the body, while he set off on horseback to inform the authorities and to summon help.

By 10.30 pm, when Police Constable Alfred Hall arrived at the scene of the 'accident', daylight was fading. The two farmworkers helped him to lift the body, along with the bicycle, onto a horse-drawn milk-cart. Later Dr Kynaston Williams arrived by car, and examined the body as best he could, noting a great deal of blood on Bella's head and some bruising and abrasions on her face, consistent with her having fallen from her bicycle. Dr Williams commented to PC Hall that, in his opinion, the girl had probably died from exhaustion or loss of blood following a sudden haemorrhage.

Bella Wright's body was taken to Little Stretton, where it was placed in a disused chapel. There, by candlelight, Dr Williams

33

Bella Wright.

made a second examination of the body but found nothing new, before driving home to Billesdon. There, matters might have ended, with the death attributed to either a sudden haemorrhage or a fatal cycling accident, had it not been for the impressive initiative of PC Alfred Hall. He was puzzled by several aspects of the accident: if the girl had bled so profusely, why was her bicycle and the coat she was wearing free of blood? It didn't quite add up.

On the next morning, Sunday 6th July, Alfred Hall returned to the chapel at Little Stretton. First he examined the bicycle and confirmed his impression that, apart from some blood on one pedal, it was unstained. He then re-examined Bella's body and discovered that in the centre of her facial bruising there was a round hole below her left eye that looked as if it had been caused by a bullet. After informing his superiors, he returned to the spot where Bella had been found and made a thorough search.

Overnight rain and the fact that the road had been reopened to traffic did not help his investigations, but he made several discoveries. He found bloodstains on the field gate near where Bella's body had been. He also made a rather macabre find: a large, black, dead bird which he called a raven, but which was probably a crow. It had apparently feasted on the large pool of human blood at the scene of the incident. PC Hall was later to inform the coroner that it had 'died by gorging itself with blood'. During his searches, Alfred Hall was later joined by the farmer Joseph Cowell, and together they found a man-made track leading from the scene of Bella's death away across the field. Then at 3 pm, PC Alfred Hall made one more tremendous discovery: a spent bullet trampled into the road by passing cattle, only 17 feet from where Bella's body had lain. The bullet was a .455 and had marks on it which suggested to the policeman that it had been fired from a revolver.

After reporting back to his superior, Sergeant Barratt, PC Hall contacted Dr Williams to tell him what had been found and to suggest that he make another examination of the body. The doctor was irritated by the policeman's comments and said that he would take a look on the next day, when he was in the area. Alfred Hall rightly said that he was not satisfied with that and would have to fetch in a different doctor. Dr Williams was there within the hour! He confirmed that the small hole below Bella's eye could have been caused by a bullet, and found a larger exit hole in the back of her head, which had been hidden by her hat and her hair. It seemed that the country policeman had been right, and that the member of the Royal College of Physicians had been wrong. Bella had been killed by being shot through the head. This was later confirmed by the coroner's inquest which returned a verdict of 'wilful murder by some person unknown'.

Although Bella's brother Philip had searched for her through Saturday night and her mother Mary had walked into Evington to report her missing on the Sunday, it was Monday before the family were told about the dead girl and were able to identify their 21 year old daughter.

More facts began to emerge about Bella's last journey. George Measures, Bella's uncle, had noticed a man in his thirties or forties 'lurking about' near his house in Gaulby while Bella was visiting on the night of her death. The man had a green bicycle with him. George, a blunt spoken roadmender, pointed him out to his niece, adding that he did not like the look of him. Bella informed her uncle that she had spoken to the man on her journey after he caught up with her on the road. He had told her that he had cycled from Great Glen, and had asked the name of the village they were approaching. Bella had laughed at her uncle's worries and assured him that if the stranger were still there when she left, she would try to give him the slip.

The man was still there at nine o'clock when Bella was leaving and he came up to speak to her. George Measures was sure that the stranger had spoken to Bella by name, saying, 'Bella, I thought you'd gone the other way home.' This was confirmed by George's son-in-law James Evans, the Yorkshire miner. James, a keen cyclist himself, took particular notice of the man's bicycle: it was a green framed BSA with an unusually sophisticated back-pedalling brake. He also observed that the gear cable was new, suggesting a recent repair.

Margaret Evans thought that the man didn't speak with a local accent but sounded more like a Londoner. Bella had not replied to the stranger, but when she set off home, pushing her cycle up the hill towards Gaulby church, the man had accompanied her. None of the family had been very happy about this, given the fact that the stranger looked much older than Bella and she was in any case 'walking out' with Archie Ward, her sailor.

However, Bella had not seemed worried or asked them to interfere. Later, of course, everyone wished they had done something different: Margaret could have asked her cousin to stay overnight, James could have cycled back to Stoughton with her, George could have 'seen the man off'.

A handbill was published by the Leicestershire Chief Constable Edward Holmes, giving the details of the man the police wanted to interview. Based on the description given by the Measures family, the missing cyclist was said to be 35 to 40 years of age, and between 5'7" and 5'9" in height. He was 'apparently usually clean shaven but had not shaved for a few days, hair turning grey, broad full face, broad build, said to have a squeaking voice and to speak in a low tone.'

His clothing was described as a light rainproof coat with green plaid lining, a grey mixture suit, grey cap, collar and tie, black boots, and cycle clips. His green BSA bicycle was described in full detail, thanks to the facts given by James Evans.

The handbill, which offered a £5 reward, was distributed to police forces throughout the country as well as to local newspapers. The press coverage soon spread to the national papers, and sensational speculative facts were soon added. The *Daily Chronicle* had Bella Wright speeding away from the man on the green bicycle, who pursued her with a gun in his hand, overtook her and then shot her. With such wide coverage, it seemed certain that the man must surely have read these accounts, wherever he was.

In Leicester, two schoolgirls came forward to say that they had been cycling on the Stretton Road at 5.30 pm on the Saturday in question when they were approached by a man who wanted to ride along with them. The girls, aged 12 and 14, were alarmed and turned back towards Leicester but the man rode alongside for a while until he had to stop to adjust some part of his cycle. His bicycle was green and their description of its handlebars matched that given by James Evans.

A farmer named Tom Nourish came forward to say that he had seen a girl and a man cycling towards Gaulby. Later, he had seen the same man 'in need of a shave' waiting around the village. Charles and Elizabeth Palmer had been delivering groceries in their van that evening; they too saw the girl and man riding towards Gaulby. When they called at George Measures'

Telephone 357 and 862.

LEICESTERSHIRE CONSTABULARY.

£5 REWARD.

At 9-20 p.m., 5th instant, the body of a woman, since identified as that of ANNIE BELLA WRIGHT, was found lying on the Burton Overy Road, Stretton Parva, with a bullet wound through the head, and her bicycle lying close by.

Shortly before the finding of the body the deceased left an adjacent village in company of a man of the following description :—

Age 35 to 40 years, height 5 ft. 7 in. to 5 ft. 9 in.; apparently usually clean shaven, but had not shaved for a few days, hair turning grey, broad full face, broad build, said to have squeaking voice and to speak in a low tone.

Dressed in light Rainproof Coat with green plaid lining, grey mixture jacket suit, grey cap, collar and tie, black boots, and wearing cycle clips.

Had bicycle of following description, viz.:—Gent's B.S.A., green enamelled frame, black mudguards, usual plated parts, up-turned handle bar, 3-speed gear, control lever on right of handle bar, lever front brake, back-pedalling brake worked from crank and of unusual pattern, open centre gear case, Brooke's saddle with spiral springs of wire cable. The 3-speed control had recently been repaired with length of new cable.

Thorough enquiries are earnestly requested at all places where bicycles are repaired.

If met with the man should be detained, and any information either of the man or the bicycle wired or telephoned to E. HOLMES, Esq., CHIEF CONSTABLE OF COUNTY, LEICESTER, or to SUPT L. BOWLEY, COUNTY POLICE STATION, LEICESTER.

County Constabulary Office,
Leicester, 7th July, 1919.

T. H. DAY & SONS, PRINTERS 7 St MARTINS LEICESTER

The 'wanted' poster.

house they were introduced to the girl as Bella Wright. They saw the man hanging around the village, a little way from the cottage.

The most useful piece of information came in immediately the handbill was published. A cycle dealer named Harry Cox, who had a shop in the Spinney Hill district of Leicester, came forward to say that he had repaired a green bicycle a few days before Bella Wright's death. The bike had been brought in on the morning of Wednesday 2nd July for a tyre repair and to have the gears adjusted. However, the gear cable broke and Harry kept the bicycle an extra day to replace it. The owner collected the machine on the Friday morning, but came in again in the afternoon asking Harry to take an inch off the new cable so that he could adjust it easily himself. This was done and the cycle was collected a second time at 2 pm on Saturday 5th July, the day Bella Wright met her death. Superintendent Levi Bowley, in charge of the murder investigation, was very interested in the fact that Harry had just described the new gear cable noticed by James Evans later that evening.

Harry Cox remembered that the man was unshaven, had a squeaky voice, and that he had ridden off eastwards towards Evington and Stoughton. Questioned further, Harry recalled the man telling him that he had not long been demobbed from the forces, and that he was in Leicester visiting friends because the London firm he was going to work for had given him some extra weeks holiday. It seemed certain that the man who had visited Harry Cox's shop was the same man who had accompanied Bella on her last cycle ride. As the green bicycle was unrideable when first brought in, it seemed probable that the man was staying somewhere within easy walking distance of Harry's shop.

The hopes raised by this early lead proved premature; no further evidence came to light, even though the reward for information was raised from £5 to £20.

It was in February 1920, seven months later, that the next breakthrough occurred. Enoch Whitehouse was a boatman-haulier working on the Leicester canals, and on 23rd February he was delivering a load of coal to a factory when the tow rope of his horse-drawn barge went slack. It dipped into the murky canal water, then tightened and came up again. Enoch hardly had time to register that a bike frame was tangled in the rope, before it fell back into the water. By an amazing piece of coincidence, the factory was Bates' Rubber Mill, where Bella had been employed up to her death!

That night, Enoch Whitehouse thought long and deep about the bicycle frame; he was sure that it had been green, the colour of the one the police were seeking. The next day, driven on either by civic duty or by thoughts of the reward, he was back on the canal bank, fishing with a grappling hook. He knew just where to look and eventually he hooked out the front wheel of a bike and a green bicycle frame. Excitedly he called over a man further along the tow path. This time the coincidence was one that any novelist would dismiss as too far-fetched. The other man on the tow path was John Ward, father of Archie Ward the sailor boy-friend of Bella Wright.

John rushed into the factory to tell his daughters Sally and Gertrude what had happened and the factory grapevine made sure that everyone in Bates' Rubber Mill soon knew that part of the green bicycle had been found. Enoch Whitehouse was in less of a hurry, and it was Friday 27th February before the cycle frame ended up on the desk of Superintendent Levi Bowley.

He wasted no time however in ordering a thorough search of the length of the canal where Enoch had made his find. A number of police officers working under Sgt Healey dragged the canal; some of their equipment was no more sophisticated than Enoch Whitehouse's grappling hook. Contemporary photographs show the police using lines with hooks on the end, and long-handled rakes. However, they did have a metal tube with a glass window in the end that made it possible to look at objects on the canal bed.

A motley crowd of onlookers gathered each day and cheered every piece of junk fished from the river. Most of the rescued debris was loaded onto a cart and taken away for examination, though the police did allow the crowd to claim the considerable amount of coal fished out.

The search of the canal went on for some weeks, and it was on 19th March that Sgt Healey fished out a leather revolver holster containing a number of .455 calibre cartridges of the same type as the one found by PC Hall at the scene of Bella Wright's death. The holster was found to be of the Army service type issued to officers. The revolver itself was never found.

The wheel and frame discovered by the canal haulier were subjected to a detailed examination, along with other parts discovered in the canal. It was soon realised that the green bicycle had been carefully dismantled and the various parts deliberately thrown into different parts of the canal. Moreover the maker's name and the machine's number had been filed away before the parts were put into the canal. It was obvious that this was not just a dumped stolen bike; someone had gone to a great deal of trouble to make the bicycle difficult to identify. However, the BSA agent in Leicester, William Saunders of the Champion Cycle Shop, managed to find a second number on the inside of the front forks.

Now that the police had the number – 103648 – they were able to approach the BSA bicycle manufacturers. Superintendent Bert Taylor went to the headquarters of BSA in Birmingham, then to the main factory in Redditch. The fact that the bicycle was a special order fitted with the unusual back brake enabled a clerk in the sales department to find a record showing that this bicycle had been supplied to a shop in Derby. Supt Taylor continued his Midlands tour, and visited the shop of Orton Brothers in Friargate, Derby. There Joseph Orton showed him the ledger recording the sale of bicycle number 103648 in May 1910 to a Mr Ronald Light. The trail which had seemed stone cold in the months after Bella's death, was now red hot again. In 1910, Ronald Light had been in lodgings in Derby but the police had little trouble in tracing the address of his mother's house in the Highfields district of Leicester.

Supt Levi Bowley visited Mrs Light and obtained the present address of her son; he had recently moved to Cheltenham to take up a post as assistant mathematics master at a private boys' school. Accompanied by a detective sergeant of the Gloucestershire constabulary, Bert Taylor went to the Dean Close School in Cheltenham on Thursday 4th March 1920. Whether Supt Bowley was impressed by the establishment is not recorded, but meeting Ronald Light for the first time must have given him a few doubts. The 34 year old teacher was confident and self assured. His appearance and clothing were smart; there was certainly no sign of the unshaven mystery man he was seeking. One thing might have reassured the Leicester police officer: Ronald Light certainly had a squeaky voice.

Questioned about the green bicycle, Light provided Supt

Ronald Light.

Taylor with a series of stories. Initially he denied ever having owned a cycle of that colour, but when he realised that the police had evidence of his purchase he changed his story, saying that he once owned a green bike but had sold it seven years earlier to someone he could not remember. Taken to Cheltenham police station, Light adjusted his story again, now saying that he had sold his green bicycle to his former landlord in Derby. Later investigation proved that the cycle sold to this man was black in colour, and was sold by Light two years before he purchased the green bicycle from Orton Brothers. Ronald Light explained the differing versions he was giving by saying that he had owned so many different cycles over the years that he could not be expected to remember what had happened to all of them. The one piece of his testimony that remained constant at this time was that he had not been anywhere near the village of Gaulby on 5th July 1919, and he had never met Bella Wright.

Harry Cox, the Leicester cycle dealer who had repaired the green bicycle just before Bella's death, was brought south to Cheltenham. He had no difficulty in picking out Ronald Light from an identity parade of nine men. Ronald Light was brought back to Leicester where he took part in a number of identity parades spread over several days. George Measures, Bella's uncle, picked him out immediately, as did James Evans, Elizabeth Palmer and the two young girls who had been approached by a man on a green bicycle a few hours before Bella's death.

Ronald Light was formally charged with the wilful murder of Bella Wright on Friday 5th March, and was remanded in custody. The police began to find out more about the man they had charged. Ronald was the only son of Catherine and the late George Light. His father had been the manager of Ellistown Colliery in Leicestershire, as well as a partner in a Birmingham manufacturing firm and an inventor of several items, including a device for extracting pen nibs, a tie holder, and a syphon system for improving the flushing of lavatories. Ronald's mother had come from a professional background, her father being a well-respected Bristol solicitor.

Ronald Light's childhood had been, by most standards, a privileged one; he had received his education at Stoneygate prep school in Leicester, followed by Oakham public school. Despite an early reputation for preferring a life of ease to one of study, he had gained a third class degree in engineering in 1912. He had worked as an engineer for the Midland Railway in Derby until the outbreak of the First World War, when he had taken a commission as Second Lieutenant in the Royal Engineers. His life as an officer had ended in August 1916 when he had been ordered to resign his commission for 'lack of initiative'. He returned to England and, without informing his family, spent a few weeks in the West Country before rejoining the war as a private in the Honourable Artillery Company.

After demobilization in February 1919, he had lived with his mother in Leicester until taking up a post as mathematics tutor in Cheltenham in January 1920. This meant that at the time of Bella Wright's death, he was resident in Leicester.

At the preliminary hearings before Alfred Turner JP, the evidence against Ronald Light was presented. There were all the witnesses who had identified him as being the man who had been with Bella Wright on the night of her death. There was the testimony proving that he was the owner of the green bicycle with the distinctive back brake, which had been disposed of in the canal. The bicycle bell and chain were not found in the canal with the other parts, but were recovered from Mrs Light's house in Leicester.

A maid, Mary Webb, who worked at Catherine Light's house gave evidence that Ronald Light normally returned from his cycle trips at 8 pm, but that on Saturday 5th July 1919, he had returned at 10 pm looking dusty and tired. Ethel Tunnicliffe, a former girl-friend of Ronald Light from his time in Derby, testified that in 1915 he had sent her a parcel containing his service revolver, asking her to take it to his mother's house in Leicester.

The only thing missing from this avalanche of circumstantial evidence was a motive; Bella had not, in the euphemistic words of the post-mortem, 'been outraged', nor had her clothing been disturbed. Indeed, when her body was found she was still wearing her hat.

Throughout all the evidence, Ronald Light appeared unruffled and calm. Pleading not guilty to the charge of murder, he reserved his defence and gave no indication of how he would set about proving his innocence. The prosecution wondered if he would try to bring forward alibi witnesses at his main trial. There was found to be a prima facie case against him, and

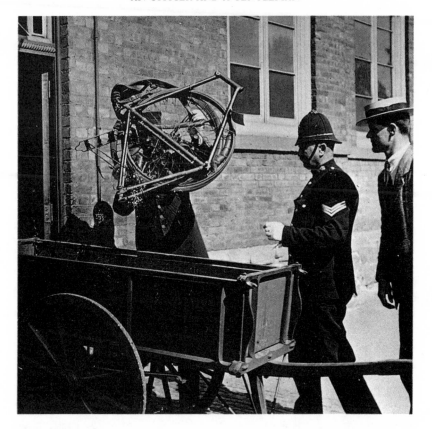

The green bicycle, which had been recovered from the canal, is carried into court. (Leicestershire Constabulary)

Ronald Light was summoned to appear before a jury at the next assizes.

The trial began on Wednesday 9th June 1920, before Judge Sir Thomas Gardner Horridge. The prosecution was led by Sir Gordon Hewitt, the Attorney General. It appears that there had been a political decision taken after the end of the Great War, that the Attorney General would take charge personally in any charge of wilful murder against a former soldier, in order to reassure the public that returning soldiers would not bring back wartime violence into civilian life. Given the catalogue of evidence against Light, and the presence of the Attorney General in the prosecution, things appeared hopeless for Light.

However, the defence was to be led by Sir Edward Marshall Hall, the leading defence lawyer of the day. He was renowned as a tough and dogged fighter for his clients, he possessed a fine voice, and would weep real tears of emotion as he pleaded for the life of the accused. No one is sure how the widow Mrs Light was able to afford the legal fees of this great defender, but it is thought by many that she was financially helped by former business friends or masonic brothers of her late husband. One amazing fact about Sir Edward's defence in this case is that when he came into court on that Wednesday morning, he had never met or spoken to Ronald Light! To a man of his ability, it was not necessary. One thing was certain however: if Light persisted with his protest that he did not own the green bicycle, even Marshall Hall could not persuade a jury to believe him.

The Attorney General opened the case for the prosecution by describing the events of the 5th July up to the point where the man on the green bicycle had ridden away from Gaulby with Bella Wright, adding, 'The evidence I have to submit to you is that that man was the prisoner, Ronald Vivian Light and that his was the hand that fired the revolver that took her life.' He pointed out that Light had purchased the green bicycle in Derby in 1910 and had ridden it regularly between then and 5th July 1919. On that date he returned home at 10.00 pm, and was never seen to ride the bicycle again. When asked by Mary Webb about his cycle he had informed her that it had been sold. Light had continued to live at his mother's house in Leicester until the time when the frame of the green cycle had been recovered from the canal.

Sir Gordon touched on the question of motive, saying that Light might have made unwelcome overtures to Bella, but pointed out that in any case it was not necessary to attribute motive in order to prove guilt. He said that the disposal of the cycle and the revolver holster had been a deliberate effort to conceal evidence, involving filing the number off the cycle before dismantling it and distributing the parts over a length of canal. He concluded by drawing attention to the untrue stories told by Light to Supt Taylor about the ownership of the green cycle.

As witnesses were called by the prosecution – Mary Wright, Joseph Cowell, George Measures, James Evans, Elizabeth Palmer,

Thomas Nourish, Kathleen Power, Harry Cox – it was noticeable that Sir Edward Marshall Hall declined to cross-question most of them, except to ask PC Hall about the size of the bullet hole in Bella Wright's face.

However, when Muriel Nunney and Valeria Cavan – the two young girls who claimed to have been pestered by Light earlier on the Saturday evening – gave their evidence, the Great Defender went to town. Noticing that their formal statements were given seven months after the event, he suggested that they had made them after reading in the newspapers about the hunt for the man with the green bicycle, and that the date of 5th July had been given to them by the police. Although they each denied this, he had succeeded in sowing seeds of doubt about their testimony.

When Dr Williams gave his evidence, he produced a gruesome exhibit: the piece of skin with the bullet hole in it which he had cut from Bella's face during the post-mortem. Marshall Hall again concentrated on the size of it, suggesting that it was too small to have been caused by the .455 bullet if fired from a revolver at close range. When the prosecution called Henry Clarke as an expert on fire-arms, Marshall Hall pressed him hard to say that the bullet that passed through Bella Wright's head must have been fired from a great distance, but Clarke would not do so. He did agree, though, that the bullet could have been fired from either a revolver or a rifle.

As the prosecution team concluded their case, Ronald Light passed his lawyer a note that was to change the course of the trial. The only witness called to the stand by the defence was the prisoner, Ronald Light! Marshall Hall began by taking Light back to his war service, confirming that he had owned a service revolver as an officer in the Royal Engineers, which he had taken with him when he returned to the war front as a private in the Artillery. He claimed that it had remained in France with other kit when he returned to England in 1918, 'suffering from deafness and shellshock'. The holster had remained in England, however. Light confirmed that the holster and ammunition recovered from the Leicester canal were his. This was the first indication to the court that Ronald Light was about to change his story dramatically.

Guided by his lawyer, Light told how, in 1919, he had brought his green bicycle down from the boxroom in his mother's house, and repaired its tyres to make it usable again. He agreed that he had taken it for repair to Harry Cox's shop, but he denied telling Cox that he was working for a firm in London. He then described going for a ride on the evening of Saturday 5th July towards Little Stretton, and meeting a young lady he now knew to be Bella Wright. She had been standing over her cycle and had called out to him, asking if he had a spanner. He had not, but checked her bicycle noticing some play in the free wheel. He could not adjust it, but had ridden on with her until they reached the next village, which she had told him was called Gaulby.

The girl had said that she was going to visit friends but would only be there for ten minutes or so. Light had interpreted that statement as an invitation to wait for her, but when she had not reappeared after 15 minutes he had started to ride back to Leicester. Immediately he had found that he had a flat tyre and had stopped to pump it up. The tyre went flat again and he had to take the tyre off and repair it. When he had done all this, it was 8.15, and he had ridden back to the cottage where he had left the girl to see if she was still there. He rode around for a short time, then saw her coming out.

Dismounting he went over and spoke to her, saying, 'Hello, you've been a long time. I thought you'd gone the other way.' Light was insistent that he had not addressed Bella by name, as had been alleged by George Measures and James Evans. He emphasised that the first time he knew the girl's name was when he read about her death in the newspapers.

He admitted that he and Bella had left Gaulby together, and had ridden together for ten minutes or so. He claimed that when he stopped to pump up his tyre again, Bella had ridden on very slowly. When he caught her up, they had discussed bicycle tyres and Bella had told him that she was able to buy them at cost price from the tyre factory where she worked. After riding past the left turn to King's Norton, the two cyclists had parted company at the next junction, with Ronald Light turning right onto the top road to Leicester and Bella Wright taking the left turn down to the Via Devana. Light stated that the reason that he did not reach Leicester until 10 pm was because he had to keep stopping to pump up his tyre.

Light claimed that the first he knew of Bella's death was when he read of it in the *Leicester Mercury* three days later. He had guessed that the dead girl was the one he had spoken to, and realised he was the man the police were seeking. His mother being on holiday in Rhyl, he was able to take the green bicycle from its usual spot in the kitchen to the boxroom at the top of the house. In the October, when the evenings were darker, he had dismantled the cycle and thrown the separate parts into the canal, along with his gun-holster and cartridges. The reason he had panicked was because the papers had all been saying that the man with the green bicycle was the murderer of Bella Wright.

The dramatic effect of this new story from Ronald Light was considerable. Under the guidance of Sir Edward Marshall Hall, he had admitted that the evidence of George Measures, James Evans, and all the other witnesses who had seen him with Bella Wright, was correct. He had concurred with all that Harry Cox had said about the repairs to his green bicycle. He had admitted that he had panicked and thrown his dismantled bicycle, his gun-holster and his cartridges into the canal. Now, all he was denying was the murder.

Suddenly, the prosecution case was different; they had been expecting to have to convince the jury that Ronald Light was the man seen with Bella, the man who owned the green bicycle. Now their task was turned around. How would the Attorney General deal with it? Amazingly, he was no longer there! He had returned to London and left the rest of the prosecution to Henry Maddocks and Norman Birkett. No one has ever been able to explain Sir Gordon Hewitt's sudden departure. It has been suggested that he was required to attend a debate in the House of Commons, though the Hansard record shows he did not speak in it.

Whatever the reason, Henry Maddocks KC, an experienced lawyer but hardly in the same league as the Attorney General, now took over the cross-questioning of Ronald Light. The first questions were about the revolver said to have been left in France. Light claimed that although he knew that as a private he could never have worn it, he took it to the front with him, though he had left its holster in Leicester. Asked about the green bicycle Light admitted that, after throwing it into the canal, he had told his mother that he had sold it. He claimed that the reasons for his action were partly through panic caused by bad nerves incurred by his war service, and also to save worrying his mother who suffered from a bad heart.

When questioned about the evidence of the two schoolgirls, Muriel Nunney and Valeria Cavan, Light continued to deny ever having met or spoken to them. Their statements were completely untrue, he insisted. He had not met them on that day or on any other. He also denied telling the cycle dealer, Harry Cox, that he was a visitor on holiday in Leicester. He admitted that the clothing he had worn on the day of Bella's death had since been 'disposed of'.

In his closing speech, Henry Maddocks pointed out that the accused man had been seen with Bella Wright half an hour before her death, and now admitted being with her about 15 minutes before the tragic event. He drew attention to Light's 'wonderful silence' when he first learned that the police were seeking the rider of the green bicycle, to which he had added deception when questioned by the police. Maddocks made clear his annoyance that Light's change of story had occurred towards the end of the trial. This had taken the prosecution by surprise, and prevented more relevant evidence – placing Light on the road where the girl had been killed, for example – being sought. It also prevented the police from searching Light's house at an early stage, to check whether the missing revolver was still in his possession in 1919.

He invited the jury, 'as men of the world', to consider the fact that Light had waited for Bella for almost an hour while she was visiting her uncle in Gaulby, and had been heard to call her by her first name. He pointed out that Light could have cycled from the place where he claimed to have parted from Bella to the murder location by taking the alternative road through Little Stretton, thus intercepting her. He contrasted Light's claim to have been dazed and confused when he read about the death with the thoroughness used in dismantling his green cycle, filing away its identification number, and disposing of the parts in the canal, together with his revolver holster and ammunition. Maddocks finished by asking the jury to consider whether these were the actions of an innocent man.

Sir Edward Marshall Hall began his closing speech by reminding the jury that they held the life of Ronald Light in their hands. All the evidence was circumstantial. If they believed that Light had lied about his identity to Harold Cox that Saturday afternoon, and had then taken his revolver with him on his evening ride, that implied that he had gone out to commit a premeditated crime against a girl he had never met before. He laid great stress on the absence of a motive for the murder. He admitted Light's foolishness and moral cowardice in remaining silent for so long, but referred to his gallant war service, pointing out that 'shell shock destroys nerve vitality'.

Marshall Hall spoke to the jury for an hour, addressing each individual juror in turn, and culminated with his well-known scales of justice performance, involving him raising his arms to represent the statue of Justice at the Old Bailey. He balanced the scales, then tilted them to show how much lighter was the prosecution case compared with that of the defence.

After the judge's summing up the jury retired and, three and a half hours later, returned a verdict of not guilty.

Ronald Light did not return to his teaching post in Cheltenham; quite apart from his involvement in the murder case, his employers found that the testimonials he used to obtain the post had been forged. Light moved to the Isle of Sheppey in Kent, and changed his name to Leonard Estelle, though he reverted to his real name in the early 1940s. A Leicestershire woman, Lilian Bowers from Ibstock, lived with him and they married in 1934. Light died in 1975 at the age of 89.

Ronald Light's acquittal on the charge of murder has always been a subject of debate. The verdict was greeted with astonishment and dismay by Kenus and Mary Wright, Bella's parents. The overwhelming judgement of Leicestershire people was that Light was 'got off' by the sheer brilliance of Sir Edward Marshall Hall, the Great Defender, although in 1982 a slim twelve page pamphlet written and published by A W P Mackintosh of Evington did defend the possibility that Bella could have been shot accidentally by someone shooting crows. He even suggests that the dead bird found by PC Hall could be evidence that bird shooting was going on at the time. This ignores PC Hall's evidence that the bird had choked after gorging on the blood at the scene. Nor does this theory explain how Bella's hat had been put back on her head, thus disguising the exit wound of the fatal bullet!

In 1993, a much more thorough and comprehensive account was published, containing new evidence about the life and character of Ronald Light. In her book, *The Green Bicycle Murder*, Wendy East provides information that was not known to the jury at the original trial.

51

In 1902, Ronald Light was expelled from Oakham public school for 'lifting a little girl's clothes over her head'. Not a serious crime of course, if the children were the same age, but the girl was very young and Light was 17 at the time. What seems a humorous incident suddenly takes on new implications. In 1914, when he was 28, Light had evidently not outgrown his childish obsessions. He was dismissed by the Midland Railway in Derby for 'making rude figures on the lavatory walls' and for setting fire to a cupboard. In 1916, Lieutenant Ronald Light was cashiered from the Royal Engineers for reasons that are unclear. 'Lack of initiative' was the official verdict, although Light's abilities as an engineer have never been questioned. In her researches, Wendy East constantly encountered rumours that the reason for Light losing his commission was connected with an alleged assault on a French postmistress.

Although this rumour is not substantiated, what is true is that on his return to Leicester in 1916, he had an affair with a local woman, telling her that his name was Davis. Later that summer, he worked on a farm in the West Country, until he was suspected of setting fire to hay-ricks. It was at this point that he rejoined the army as a gunner, with the rank of private. In 1917, he faced a courtmartial for forging telegraphic orders and for wearing medals to which he was not entitled; he was sentenced to a year's detention. In the same year, he was struck from the register of the Institution of Civil Engineers.

In 1918, while a patient being treated for deafness at Wharn-cliffe Hospital, Light made sexual advances to the 15 year old daughter of an ambulance driver who had befriended him and invited him to his house. In October 1919, after the death of Bella Wright but before his arrest, Ronald Light was taken to the Clarendon Road police station in Leicester, accused of sexually molesting an eight year old girl. At first, Light denied the offence but he later admitted it and apologised. The girl's parents decided not to press charges, and Light was allowed to go free.

Some of the evidence about Ronald Light's character may be peripheral or unsubstantiated, but it hardly squares with the picture of 'an officer and a gentleman' portrayed by some of the press during the trial. One national newspaper referred to him throughout as Lieutenant Light, although he had suddenly ceased to be entitled to that rank in 1916.

However, the accumulation of proven facts about him is very telling. It is certainly impossible to disagree with Wendy East when she says that far more significance should have been given to the two schoolgirls who claimed to have been approached by Ronald Light on the night of the murder.

Appearing on the ITV programme *Crime Stalker* on 5th May 1994, Wendy East put forward evidence that Bella Wright had told Gertrude and Sally Ward that a soldier had on several occasions waited for her when she was out cycling, and had engaged her in conversation. Bella had even pointed the man out to the Ward sisters when they saw him once in Leicester. Unfortunately, although the sisters informed the police about the matter, they were never called to identify the man in court. John Stalker, the former Assistant Chief Constable of Manchester and a very experienced detective, said that had a jury been in possession of the additional facts, it seems probable that the verdict would have been different.

Perhaps those Leicestershire locals of the time who thought and said that the Great Defender had helped 'the-bloke-as-done-it' get away with it, were not just partisan country bumpkins. After all, it had been a country police constable who had shown enough initiative to prevent the death of Bella Wright being recorded as due to a cycling accident, in the first place.

5

THE TAXICAB MURDER

THE MURDER OF JOAN HENSON AT LEICESTER,
JANUARY 1948

A newspaper report in the *Leicester Mercury* on 26th January
1948 told how, in one room of the Leicester Royal Infirmary, there lay Squadron Leader Josef Zawadski of the Polish Air
Force, suffering from gunshot wounds to the head. At the same
time, in another room of the same building, an inquest was being
held into the death of a 27 year old woman. The coroner, Mr E
G B Fowler, said that the dead woman's name was Mrs Frances
Joan Minns but that she was known locally by her maiden name,
Joan Henson. Detective Superintendent Haywood told the inquest
that it was anticipated that someone would be brought before the
court during the coming week.

The death of Joan Henson and the wounding of the Polish Air
Force officer were connected to a dramatic incident that had
taken place in a taxicab at 2 pm on Saturday 24th January 1948.
The taxi had been called to the Grand Hotel to convey two pas-
sengers, a man and a woman, to an address in Kitchener Road.
Before they reached the destination, the man gave the driver a £1
note, telling him that it would cover the fare and the tip.

The driver, Frank Timson, was delighted, as the fare would
have been about four shillings. The passenger had given him a
tip that was four times as much as the fare! Frank's delight
turned to horror, however, when he turned his head and saw that
the man had a gun in his right hand, a pistol that was pointing
at his fellow passenger. The armed man turned back to Frank
and handed him a bundle of seven more £1 notes, saying, 'When
we get there, fetch the police.' He then added, 'There are some
letters in my pocket.'

When the taxi arrived at its destination, 200 Kitchener Road,
the woman passenger rose from her seat, saying, 'I don't care.

I'm not frightened.' Frank saw the man fire his gun three or four times into the woman at point blank range. She groaned and fell from the taxi, landing on the pavement. At this point the man raised the gun to his own temple and two further shots rang out. As the man slumped back into the rear seat of the taxi, Frank rushed into the house. Inside, he found a lodger, Mr Shakespeare, and told him to send for the police and an ambulance.

When Frank Timson and Mr Shakespeare returned to the road outside the body of the woman was still lying on the pavement, but the injured man was stepping out of the taxi with the pistol still in his hand. He handed three letters to Frank and told him, 'I have shot her five times and tried to kill myself twice.' He continued to say that he would shoot himself again, and was trying to put another bullet into the gun – a Mauser automatic, when the police arrived. Police Inspector Harold Toach and Sergeant William Joiner approached the armed man, who said to them, 'All right, I killed her. Now I kill myself.'

Before he could have another attempt at shooting himself, Inspector Toach courageously reached out and disarmed him. After being cautioned, the injured man – Josef Zawadski – stated, 'It is finished.' Taking the three letters back from the taxi driver, Josef handed them to the police, saying, 'Please take these letters and tell her mother that I killed her. I have shot myself twice but I am not dead.' One of the letters was addressed to the police, another to Josef's commanding officer, and the third to Kathryn Henson, the dead woman's mother.

The injured man was taken to the Leicester Royal Infirmary in a police van. On the journey, he said to the police officers, 'I told her as she got out of the cab that I would kill her,' and repeated that he had tried twice to shoot himself.

The injured Josef Zawadski was examined in Leicester Royal Infirmary by Dr Violet Fox Wilkins. He was bleeding from a wound in his right temple but the wounds were not serious. When he first came round in hospital he could not recall the events that had brought him there, until he was shown a newspaper account, which brought memories flooding back. Josef told PC Arthur Smith 'She is absolutely dead, isn't she? I am glad. Now I am ready to die. It was a murder of the heart.' Later he stated, 'I want to be shot like a Polish gentleman, not hung.'

The body of the dead woman – Joan Henson – was taken to

Squadron Leader Josef Zawadski. (Leicester Mercury)

the city mortuary where it was examined by police surgeon Dr James Stewart Mann at approximately 3 pm. He found nine wounds in all, including several bullet wounds evident in the upper body and the left arm. One bullet had passed through the upper arm, then penetrated the chest, another had entered the chest directly. The heart showed two perforated wounds and the surgeon concluded that death must have occurred instantaneously. There was also slight bruising to both legs below the knees. Answering a later question from the inquest jury, Dr Mann explained that the bruising would not have been caused by a struggle but would have occurred when the dead woman fell from the taxi.

After delivering their injured passenger to hospital and sending the woman's body to the mortuary, the police began to put together their tragic story. Joan Henson had spent her childhood in Canada, before coming to England with her parents. She was working in an office in Leicester until 1939 when, at the age of 18, she married Henry Minns. Henry was a paint merchant manager, but when the Second World War broke out he was called up into the army. Joan's younger sister had married an American serviceman and left Leicester as a GI bride.

In August 1942, while her husband was serving abroad, Joan had met the handsome Polish Air Force officer, Squadron Leader Josef Zawadski, and had fallen in love with him. Josef told her straight away that he had been married but that his German wife had deserted him, though Joan did not reveal that she too had been married. The two soon became lovers and lived together as man and wife, Joan reverting to her maiden name of Henson.

They seemed very happy together, and Josef got on very well with Joan's widowed mother, Kathryn, who regarded him as a kind and caring man with perfect manners – a real gentleman. Certainly Josef was always generous, making Joan an allowance of £10 per week, an impressively large sum in the 1940s. In May 1946, Josef and Joan had a baby son, Andrew, who soon became the apple of his father's eye. Even the news that Joan had been married, discovered when Henry Minns sued for a divorce in 1946 naming Josef Zawadski as co-respondent, did not make Zawadski think any the less of his beloved Joan. He loved her and was devoted to Andrew, their young son.

The happy relationship seemed to have deteriorated in the

summer of 1947. Joan left her son with her mother and went into lodgings in Kitchener Road. Kathryn was very unhappy with her daughter's decision, and Josef Zawadski was devastated. He had delayed his repatriation to Poland in the hope and the firm belief that when he did go home he would be accompanied by Joan and Andrew. Now he found out that Joan was seeing a number of other men and living in a house with a bad reputation. He discovered that she was keeping company with a woman whom he believed to be a prostitute. His life was falling apart.

Joan, who was a qualified stenographer and a former member of the ATS, began a new job as a supervisor-receptionist at the Turkey Cafe in Granby Street a few weeks before her death. A fellow supervisor, Mrs Major, found Joan a very pleasant colleague with a likeable easy-going manner.

On the evening of Friday January 23rd, Josef called at Kathryn Henson's house in Dersingham Road. She still thought of him as a friend and a good man, and was very concerned at his stressed state. He played with Andrew for a while but refused to stay for a meal. He told Kathryn that he had an appointment to meet Joan the next day at the Grand Hotel in Leicester, and he was going to beg her to come back to him for Andrew's sake.

Joan Henson kept her appointment with her former lover at the Grand Hotel, but spurned his pleas to return to live with him and Andrew. Josef begged her to come back to her mother's house to see their son instead of going to her lodgings in Kitchener Road. When he showed her three letters he had written threatening to kill her and then commit suicide, she remained unimpressed. When he produced a gun, she told him to shoot himself with it. In the taxi he continued to ask her to change her mind, and also threatened to kill her, but Joan said that she didn't care. When the taxi arrived at Joan's lodgings in Kitchener Road, she began to get out. Realising that she was about to leave him for good, Josef shot her and tried to shoot himself.

Joan Henson's funeral service, conducted by the Rev James Adams, was held at Welford Road cemetery on the morning of Wednesday 28th January, the time and place being kept secret from the press. There were only two wreaths, one from her mother, sister and brothers, and the other from an aunt and uncle. There were just eight mourners, all close relatives.

The trial of Josef Zawadski began on Monday 15th March,

before Mr Justice Cassels, with C L Henderson, KC, leading the prosecution. Squadron Leader Zawadski, dressed in a smart blue civilian suit, stood rigidly to attention as he pleaded not guilty to the murder on the grounds that he was not sane at the time he committed the act.

The facts of what took place on 24th January were presented by the prosecution, and were not disputed by the defence. Two of the three letters written by Josef Zawadski were produced. The letter to the police was short and formal, reading: 'Dear Sirs, Sorry to be trouble, but it cannot be helped. I shall kill her, Mrs Zawadski, for personal reasons. I shall kill myself. Yours faithfully....' The letter he sent to Kathryn Henson was a little longer and much more moving: 'Darling Mummy, Terribly sorry there cannot be another way. I shall kill her and myself and finish my tortures. As I expected, she is not even coming to see me. Please arrange something for Andrew's future. Sorry I cannot do that. Cannot live any longer. There may be some money for Andrew at my station. Try and get it. Thanks very much for everything. You were always so nice to me. Josef.'

Zawadski was asked about his motive for showing the letters to Joan Henson in the Grand Hotel lounge on the afternoon of her death. He replied that he thought that they would make her want to come back to her baby. He had wanted her to read them and then destroy them.

Arthur Ward, KC, the leading defence barrister took the jury back through Josef's life. He described the blow Josef had suffered when his German wife left him, and how he had concentrated on his Air Force career. He listed Josef's awards: the Virtute Militari (equivalent to the VC), a Cross of Valour with three bars, and the Polish Air Force medal with two bars. He told the jury that Josef had become one of the most brilliant flying officers of the Polish Air Force, with wartime service in operations over Germany, Belgium, Holland and Italy. He claimed that Josef had suffered from mental blackouts over a number of years.

Wing Commander D A Upton, Josef Zawadski's commanding officer, said that he thought Josef was in a 'pretty bad way' lately, compared with his normal demeanour, and was 'mentally worried and shaken'.

Mrs Kathryn Henson, the mother of the dead woman, described the mental stress Josef had shown when he found out that Joan was seeing other men. She described Josef as a devoted father and said that he was very generous to Joan when they lived together.

Dr Arthur Colahan, a Leicester neurologist with 29 years' experience of specialist practice, said that he believed Zawadski to be suffering from a disorder of the mind known as manic depressive insanity at the time of the alleged murder. In his opinion, Josef would not have known what he did in the taxi was wrong. He also stated that jealousy played no part in Zawadski's actions; the emotion involved was an obsession about the welfare of his son.

The jury had to balance this against the evidence of Dr A B Graying, the medical officer at Leicester prison, who said that he believed Zawadski was normal and knew what he was doing at the time he fired the shots.

When the judge summed up, he outlined the facts about the events, which were not disputed. He reminded the jury that they were not a court of morals, and their opinion about Joan Henson's possible drifting into a life of prostitution and her neglect of her child was irrelevant. He acknowledged what Josef Zawadski had done for civilisation in his war service, but then launched into a xenophobic speech, saying that 'shootings and the use of knives are contrary to our British natures.' He did not explain what relevance the reference to the use of knives had to a case where no knives had been used.

The jury of eleven men and one woman retired, and brought in a verdict that Josef Zawadski was guilty but insane. He was sentenced to be detained during His Majesty's pleasure.

Perhaps the final word should be that of Kathryn Henson. Speaking of her daughter's killer she said, 'The trouble was he loved her too much. He had a pleasing personality and perfect manners. I can't think what could have gone wrong.'

6

THE HAVE-A-GO HERO

THE KILLING OF AUGUST PULKA AT LEICESTER,
AUGUST 1966

Most people have, at some time, asked themselves whether they would 'have a go' if they saw a crime being committed. If it were a bank robbery, we might excuse ourselves on the grounds that (a) banks are wealthy and well insured, and (b) the robbers are likely to be armed. Much more sensible to find a phonebox and dial 999. But what would we do if we witnessed someone being physically attacked in the street? Ignore it on the pretext that it was nothing to do with us? Go and look for a phone? Or try to intervene? Whichever we chose, and it would probably depend on whether anger or fear was our predominant emotion, we would have to live with the decision on our conscience.

Another factor might be our age and state of health, but for 74 year old August Pulka these did not enter into the reckoning. As he walked along Evington Road in Leicester at 3.30 pm on 12th August 1966, he saw a young woman being assaulted by a man and crying out for help. Despite the fact that he had scars on his brain from previous strokes and an enlarged heart he did not hesitate, but went immediately to intervene. As he approached the man committing the assault, August waved his hand at him. The man turned and struck Mr Pulka in the face, causing him to fall back on the pavement. There was a loud crack, and a pool of blood spread from August Pulka's nose and mouth.

As the young woman knelt down to help her rescuer, the offender went over to a companion standing nearby and spoke to him. The two of them left the scene. A passer-by, Mrs Margaret Devers, came over to the girl and the injured man. She later reported that the girl was covered in blood herself, and was trying to help her rescuer. In a gutter close by was a discarded melon. Lew Granville was working nearby when he was summoned to give first aid, but when he arrived at the scene he could see that the old gentleman was dead. A doctor and the police attended, and the body of August Pulka was taken to the mortuary where a post-mortem was conducted by Dr E M Ward.

The police search for the man who had assaulted the woman and struck her rescuer soon took them to a nearby greengrocer's shop, where shopkeeper Roland Orson described how two men had earlier argued over the price of a melon, an egg and an apple. The pair, who appeared to have been drinking, said they had no money, but later paid two shillings and eightpence for the items.

The police also interviewed the young woman, 24 year old Ann Montgomery. She told them that she had been going shopping when she saw two men approaching. One of them had accosted her, pinning her against a tree. She had tried to push him away, but was not strong enough to do so. She continued, 'The old gentleman came up and put his hand out and was going to say something but he didn't get a chance. The man let me go and swung his hand into the old man's face. The old man fell down on to the pavement and there was a loud crack. There was blood everywhere.' Ann told the police that the second man had walked on when she was accosted and had not participated in the assault.

It did not take the police long to find this second man, and to bring him in for questioning. James Davies told the police that he had known John Murphy for about four weeks. On 12th August they had gone for a drink, and had consumed eight pints of beer. As they walked along Evington Road, Murphy had said, 'This looks a good crack,' and had seized a girl passing by. As he struggled with her, an old man came over. Murphy's arm went out and the old man fell to the ground, hitting his head. Davies said that he had walked on, and when Murphy caught up with him, he had asked why he had done it but had received no reply. Murphy had just said that he was leaving Leicester, adding, 'You won't say anything about this, will you?'

The police now had a good description of Murphy: 5' 9" tall, with blue eyes and brown curly hair. He had an anchor and clasped hands tattooed on his left forearm, scars on his left temple and the left side of his neck, and a wart on his throat.

On 31st August, police in Bath arrested a man for assault. He had asked a girl on a bus for a kiss, then broken the nose of her boyfriend when he had objected. Although the arrested man was named Michael Buckley, his description matched that of John Murphy. A Leicestershire police officer went to Bath and found that Buckley was indeed the man known in Leicester as Murphy.

Michael Buckley was charged with the unlawful killing of August Pulka, as well as assaulting Ann Montgomery. He also faced a third charge of committing grievous bodily harm on the young man in Bath. At his trial at Leicester assizes in November 1966, Buckley said, 'Honest to God, I didn't mean to kill him. I am truly sorry for what I did to that man. I was drunk. Since I left my wife I have been on the beer and sleeping out. I didn't know he was that old, I was so drunk. I am really and truly sorry. I am sorry from my heart.'

Buckley was found guilty on the three charges, and was sentenced to four years in prison. Sentencing him, Mr Justice Mocatta said, 'When you are drunk, you are not only dangerous but you are extremely offensive to women.' Commenting on August Pulka's brave intervention the judge said, 'This was the action of a very brave man. His action prevented what could have been a serious assault on a young woman by a strong and active man 40 years his junior.'

Tributes to the courage of August Pulka, a former Polish serviceman and policeman, came from ordinary people all over the city and county. Mrs Kathleen Beaman of the Bell Inn, Frisby on the Wreake held a sale of jewellery and ladies' hats to raise money for August Pulka's widow, Emilia.

In March 1967, Mrs Emilia Pulka was invited to attend a meeting of Leicester City Council, where the Lord Mayor presented her with a certificate of commendation for bravery awarded posthumously to her husband by the Association of Chief Police Officers. The citation praised August Pulka for the unselfish way he had gone to the woman's aid and tackled a strong man many years his junior, despite his own restricted physical capabilities.

7

THE DEATH OF A GOOD SAMARITAN

THE MURDER OF MOSES HEAL AT ELLISTOWN, FEBRUARY 1973

Moses Heal, invariably known as Fred, was a good sort. He would always help out workmates with welfare problems at the Vauxhall Motors in Luton where he was employed as a paint inspector. When driving, the 59 year old Good Samaritan would often give a lift to students or servicemen. According to his son-in-law, Moses would drive up to 15 miles out of his way to take hitch-hikers to their destination, or to where they could get another lift. It was this generous nature that was to lead to his death.

It was 2 pm on 23rd February 1973 when Moses said goodbye to his wife, and set off from his home in Luton to drive up to Sunderland to see his ailing sister. He could not have stayed very long, because later the same day he rang home to say he was setting out on the return journey and expected to be back in Luton about midnight. As he drove south, Moses noticed a soldier at the side of the road with his thumb outstretched. As usual the good Samaritan pulled over to pick up the hitch-hiker.

Moses Heal never arrived home, and his worried family – concerned that he might be suffering from loss of memory – soon reported his disappearance to the police. They took the case very seriously, and a massive search began. Thousands of leaflets describing the missing man and his car – a dark blue Vauxhall Victor with the registration number YWR 828G – were printed. These were distributed to car dealers, petrol stations and other police forces.

By late March, the search was being concentrated in the fields and ditches along the M1 motorway in Leicestershire. Interest-

ingly, the 20 police officers of the Leicester and Rutland Constabulary were accompanied by a number of senior officers from
Hampshire CID, led by Detective Superintendent White. They
seemed to know where to look.

On Friday 30th March, the body of Moses Heal was found in
an advanced state of decomposition in a ditch by a farm track
between the villages of Ellistown and Battleflat. The track led to
a 100 acre mixed farm, Battleflat Farm, belonging to a Mr O T
Lees. Mr Lees had been living in a caravan at the time while the
farmhouse was being rebuilt. Although the track had been used
daily by both the farmer and the builders, they had not spotted
the body which was covered in undergrowth.

Dr Alan Usher, a Home Office pathologist, inspected the body
before it was taken away for a post-mortem. It was found that
Moses Heal had multiple injuries to the head, and his throat had
been cut. Detective Chief Superintendent Jack Broughton, of the
Leicestershire and Rutland Constabulary, showed clothing and
other items found on the dead man to Moses' son-in-law, Cyril
French. Mr French, a Luton bank official, identified them as
belonging to Mr Heal.

On Monday 2nd April 1973, an 18 year old paratrooper
appeared in court in the neighbouring town of Coalville. Andrew
Nixon, of Mons Barracks, Aldershot, was charged with the
murder of Moses Heal at Ellistown on 24th February. Details of
the discovery of the body were given by Detective Superintendent
Chris Owen, and Nixon was remanded in custody. He made
several further court appearances in Coalville, and in May Nixon
was further charged with robbing Moses Heal of £502 worth of
items, including a car, keys and documents.

It was not until October, when Andrew Nixon faced a crown
court trial before Mr Justice Geoffrey Lane, that facts came out
explaining the presence of the Hampshire police officers in the
search for Moses Heal's body in the Leicestershire countryside. It
emerged that a minor parking offence had been the key to
solving the whole case. On 26th March, a Hampshire policeman
had noticed a car illegally parked on double yellow lines in Wellington Street, Aldershot. He had also observed that the car, a
Vauxhall Victor, was displaying an excise licence which appeared
to have been altered. Although the number plate had been
changed, it was soon found that the car was that belonging to

the missing Moses Heal. The driver of the car, Andrew Nixon, was taken to the police station and searched. Documents belonging to Moses Heal were found on him, and Nixon initially claimed that Heal was his grandfather. When the police pointed out that Moses Heal was on the list of missing persons, Nixon tried to maintain his claim to be Heal's grandson, but later he made a series of admissions. These admissions led directly to a number of Hampshire detectives travelling to Leicestershire to assist with the search for Moses Heal's body.

In court, Andrew Nixon said that on the night of 23rd February he had been hitch-hiking from his home in Jarrow, County Durham, back to his barracks in Aldershot. He alleged that after Moses Heal had given him a lift, the Good Samaritan had begun to make homosexual advances, putting his hand on the young soldier's knee. His version of the events continued with Moses Heal leaving the M1 motorway, saying that he would take the hitch-hiker to the A1 where he would be more likely to get a lift to Aldershot.

However, he had driven into the farm track near Ellistown, stopped, then jumped on top of the young soldier, trying to remove his trousers. Nixon claimed that he had managed to roll the older man over, and began to hit him. After punching him 14 or 15 times, he had driven off in the man's car.

At this point the prosecution read out the pathologist's post-mortem report: 'The man had been the victim of a frenzied attack by someone using an edged weapon.' Asked how this was compatible with his own account, Nixon changed his story and admitted that he had hit Moses Heal with a brick. He also stated that after he had stopped punching Heal, he had only then realised that he had his army clasp knife in his hand. Nixon said he had shaken Heal a few times, but had panicked when there was no response. He said that at the time of the killing he was in a state of 'shock, fear and temper'. Although the temper had disappeared, the shock and fear had remained with him as he drove away.

Questioned by the prosecution, the soldier admitted that he had used the stolen vehicle, with false number plates, for almost five weeks before being arrested. Nixon's story of killing Moses Heal in the process of 'defending his honour' was further undermined when Superintendent White of the Hampshire CID gave evidence that Nixon had confessed to him: 'Yes, I did kill him. I was desperate for a car.'

The jury brought in guilty verdicts on both the charge of murder and of robbery. The judge sentenced Andrew Nixon to life imprisonment for the murder, and to 15 years for robbery, adding, 'I regard you as a callous and dangerous man.'

Perhaps the final words on Moses Heal should be those of his daughter: 'We told him it was foolish to give lifts, but he trusted mankind. He wouldn't hurt a fly.'

8

THE WEST KNIGHTON GUN SIEGE

THE MANSLAUGHTER OF ENID CABANUIK, BRIAN DAWSON AND
TERENCE WILKINSON AT LEICESTER,
SEPTEMBER 1975

L ambourne Road is a quiet street of semi-detached houses in the highly respectable West Knighton area of Leicester, but on the evening of 1st September 1975 all hell broke loose there. At half past ten, a car pulled up outside a house where three women stood talking. They were Mrs Berta 'Betty' Nikoloff of 25 Lambourne Road, Mrs Winifred Shenton of number 27, and Mrs Enid Cabanuik from number 35. A man got out of the car and began to shout abuse at them. He walked to the rear of his car, opened the boot and took out a can of petrol and a double-barrelled shotgun. As he raised the gun to fire at the women, Betty Nikoloff recognised her ex-husband Sabi whom she had recently divorced after a violent marriage.

One of the women fell to the ground, dead. The second woman hid behind a wall, while Mrs Nikoloff ran into her house, locking the door behind her. She ran upstairs and barricaded herself in a bedroom with her ten year old son, Bruno.

Teenager Stuart Shenton was walking home when he heard the shot and saw one woman fall to the ground. Thinking it was his mother who had been hit, Stuart ran towards the gunman shouting abuse at him. He ripped off his jacket and threw it at the man. Stuart then found that the woman on the ground was Mrs Cabanuik, and that his mother was hiding behind a wall. He quickly joined her.

Meanwhile the gunman - Sabi Nikoloff - had broken the window of 25 Lambourne Road and had climbed in, in pursuit of his ex-wife. He climbed the stairs pouring petrol behind him, then lit it to stop anyone following him. Inside the bedroom, Betty Nikoloff had opened the window and was crying out for help.

Neighbours who had heard the commotion came out to see what was happening. Tom Dickman, a postman who lived at number 13, helped Stuart Shenton to drag the body of Enid Cabanuik into a drive two doors away. Three of the other neighbours happened to be off-duty policemen. PC Don Acton rushed back into his house and told his wife to dial 999 and ask for the police and ambulance. Seeing the flames coming from number 25, he added the fire service to the list.

He then rejoined his off-duty colleagues John Proudman and Joe Gaughan. Together with Jeno Back – a former freedom fighter from Hungary – they managed to get a ladder up to the bedroom window where Mrs Nikoloff and Bruno were trapped. Jeno later said, 'When I came out of my house, I could hear a woman shouting from the upstairs window. Somebody had found a ladder and I just grabbed it and dashed across to the house. Bruno came down first and then his mother. I saw the chap coming towards the upstairs window and I scarpered.' The chap coming to the window was of course Sabi Nikoloff, and he was armed with his shotgun.

By this time two police cars had arrived. First on the scene were PC Alan Christian and PC James Galloway who arrived in a traffic patrol car. They parked on Lambourne Road. Finding that Mrs Cabanuik was dead, the police officers tried to force their way into the siege house by the back door. An ambulance crewed by Terry Wilkinson and Gerald Oakley had arrived, as had a divisional police car containing Sergeant Brian Dawson and PC Margaret Dayman. As these two police officers stood taking stock of the situation and being briefed by Don Acton, shots rang out from the upstairs window of 25 Lambourne Road. Brian Dawson – always known to his colleagues as Geordie – fell to the ground fatally wounded in the abdomen, while Margaret Dayman received serious gunshot wounds in her back.

Alan Christian and James Galloway returned to the front of the house, one taking cover behind a police car, the other behind the ambulance. With the help of local resident John Thomas and off-duty policeman John Proudman, they decided that they would push the ambulance towards the house to try to pick up the casualties, keeping the vehicle between themselves and the gunman. This seemed to work well. Once the ambulance was in position, they needed to get the casualties into it. With tremendous courage, Terry Wilkinson stepped out and opened the back doors. As he did so, more shots rang out and Terry fell dead, shot through the heart and right lung. At the same time, John Proudman was also injured.

PC Alan Christian tried unsuccessfully to summon help on the ambulance radio, then dashed 15 feet over to his police car. As he started to speak into the car radio, he too was shot. Fourteen year old Stuart Shenton recalled, 'I was crouching down right next to him. Suddenly he shouted, "Oh my God, I think I've been hit!" Then I saw the blood pouring out of his head. He just had enough strength to dash over to the side of the road. He was leaning over a fence and they came and took him back down the road.'

Tom Dickman, who had earlier shown great courage in pulling Mrs Cabanuik's body away from the siege house, now went over to the ambulance to help try to rescue the injured Sgt Geordie Dawson and PC Margaret Dayman. In return for his pains he received a gunshot wound in his hand.

By this time senior police officers had arrived on the scene. These included Chief Constable Alan Goodson, Assistant Chief Constable John Orme, Chief Superintendent Peter Joslin, and Superintendents Albert Driver, Eric Wright and William McGrory. Dog handlers and armed police officers were sent through the back gardens of neighbouring houses. The siege house was soon completely surrounded by uniformed officers and detectives. Fireman Mick Poulton volunteered to reverse his fire engine across the front of the house, to act as a shield for police, ambulancemen and firemen, so that they could reach the casualties. The police were preparing to fire CS gas into every room of the house. Armed police officers in flak jackets and respirators were ready to launch a simultaneous assault.

However, before the attack could be ordered, the figure of Sabi Nikoloff appeared at the front bedroom window. The fire he had lit earlier had suddenly sprung into life again, forcing him out. As he climbed over the upstairs window sill, police officers shouted to him to drop his gun. The shotgun clattered to the ground below and went off. Immediately Nikoloff dropped from

The gun siege house in Lambourne Road, West Knighton. (David Bell)

the window on top of it, but before he could pick it up he was seized by Alan Goodson and John Orme. He had actually been arrested by the county's Chief and Assistant Chief Constables. It was five minutes to midnight; the siege had lasted almost 90 minutes.

Floodlights were set up, the wounded were taken to hospital, and the bodies of Mrs Cabanuik, Sgt Geordie Dawson and ambulanceman Terry Wilkinson were examined by Home Office pathologist Dr Victor Pugh. Don Acton returned to his home, and he and his wife opened an impromptu canteen where colleagues and neighbours could share their grief and talk about their shock over cups of coffee and tea.

Those injured at the siege were taken to Leicester Royal Infirmary to have their wounds seen to. Gerald Oakley, who had driven the ambulance to Lambourne Road, insisted on leaving after his treatment to complete his shift. PC Margaret Dayman remained on the danger list for three days with injuries to her back and lungs.

Sabi Nikoloff was also taken to the hospital with slight burns to his hands. In broken English, he told the police officer accompanying him, 'You are too good to me after I done such a terrible thing. I get my gun and I shoot her. I shoot radio in car. I burn house. I do terrible things.' The police officer's reply, if he made one, is not recorded but he must surely have concurred.

At 35 Lambourne Road, the Cabanuik family mourned the loss of a wife and mother. Enid Cabanuik, a Leicester University catering supervisor, was well known throughout West Knighton as the sort of kind neighbour who would help anyone who was in difficulty.

The ambulance service mourned the tragic death of siege hero Terry Wilkinson, a 32 year old father of two from Braunstone, while the police force was grieved and shocked by the death of Geordie Dawson, a popular Newcastle-born officer who had served in Leicester for 18 years. The people of Lambourne Road, the police force and the ambulance service were not alone in their grief; the whole of Leicester and Leicestershire mourned the three deaths.

Tributes to the two men began to pour in. Deputy Station Officer John Rockley said of Terry Wilkinson, 'He was a fine ambulanceman, always a cheerful type and always ready to help you out if he could. He had looked forward to promotion and he enjoyed his work.' Crewmates described a happy-go-lucky man whose interests were largely based on his home and family. He grew cacti, and liked listening to records of the Spinners, the Liverpool folk group. He was a great radio enthusiast, and had been hoping to gain a radio transmitting licence in the near future. Colleague Bob Wright described Terry as 'a quiet family bloke,' adding, 'We were in some tough situations together, but he always escaped unscathed – until now.'

DI Roger Whitworth, a personal friend and neighbour of Geordie Dawson, described him as 'one of the nicest men I have ever met. He would always give a good word about anyone as opposed to a bad one. He would do anything for anyone, despite the pressure on his time. I never once saw him lose his temper. He had that main quality of all good policemen – an even temperament.' Writing from Canada, Mountie Ken Smith said, 'I served with the Leicestershire and Rutland Constabulary for five years, and one of the most pleasing things that arose out of my service was my friendship with Geordie Dawson.' Another colleague stated, 'He was a big man and a deep thinker. There are quite a few kids about who could have been before a juvenile court, but who were put on the straight and narrow because he got involved.'

Sergeant Dawson's funeral service took place at Leicester Cathedral and was conducted by the Provost, the Very Rev John Hughes. The cathedral was packed with family, friends, neighbours and colleagues, including Mrs Lily Marriott (the Lord Mayor of Leicester), the Duke of Rutland (chairman of the County Council) and Colonel P H Lloyd (chairman of the county Police Authority). The address was given by Chief Constable Alan Goodson, who paid tribute to Sgt Dawson's total commitment to serving the community with the words, 'Brian Dawson was doing his duty, helping others as he always had, when he died. We in the police force mourn the loss of a brave colleague and a true policeman.'

Sabi Nikoloff, a 50 year old naturalised Briton born in Bulgaria, made a three minute appearance in court on 3rd September, where he was charged with the murders of Enid Cabanuik, Brian Dawson and Terence Wilkinson. He was granted legal aid, but made no application for bail. He was remanded in custody. At later hearings, he was also charged with the attempted murder of Winifred Shenton, Margaret Dayman, Gerald Oakley and Alan Christian. In addition he faced charges of wounding Thomas Dickman with intent to do him grievous bodily harm, and endangering the lives of Berta and Bruno Nikoloff by setting fire to the house at 25 Lambourne Road.

The full trial took place in February 1976. Speaking through an interpreter, Sabi Nikoloff pleaded not guilty to the three murders, but guilty to the manslaughter of all three on the grounds of diminished responsibility. He pleaded guilty to all the other charges with the exception of the attempted murder of PC Christian. The prosecution counsel, David Smout QC, said that in view of the medical evidence he accepted Nikoloff's pleas, and that the charge relating to PC Christian should 'be allowed to lie on the files'.

Outlining the events that had led to the tragedy on 1st September, David Smout described how the marriage of Sabi and Berta Nikoloff had been a violent one, ending in divorce. He said that Nikoloff had been outraged when the divorce court ordered him to give up his claim to the house at 25 Lambourne Road. He was also bitter against Enid Cabanuik who had given evidence against him during the divorce proceedings. On the night of 1st September he had been driving along Lambourne Road, when he saw his former wife talking at her gate with Mrs Cabanuik and another woman. The three women were laughing together, and he became convinced they were laughing at him. In a rage, he had driven round the corner to his lodgings in Shackerdale Road to fetch a can of fuel and a double-barrelled shotgun. He had returned to Lambourne Road, shot Mrs Cabanuik dead at point blank range, and tried to shoot the other neighbour. He had pursued his ex-wife into the house, and set fire to the stairs. By the time he broke into the front bedroom, Mrs Nikoloff and her son had escaped down a ladder.

A statement made by Sabi Nikoloff to the police was quoted. 'I go to Lambourne Road and these two women and my wife standing outside my house. They laughing at me. I go past again and stop my car. Me angry at them laughing. They ruin my life. I take gun from boot and shoot at women. I no care if I kill her. I want to punish her for ruining my life.' When the police asked if he knew what he was doing, he replied, 'Sure.' However when asked about shooting at the police officers and ambulance crew, Nikoloff answered, 'I no do that. I shoot at shadows when they move.' David Smout said that throughout the interview, Nikoloff had continuously confessed, 'I fire plenty.'

The defence counsel, Michael Parker QC, said that three of the four doctors who had examined Sabi Nikoloff had diagnosed him as seriously mentally ill and in need of treatment. Psychiatrist Dr Peter Noble gave evidence that when he examined the defendant in prison, he had concluded that he was paranoid with delusions of persecution. He said that Nikoloff felt that his former neighbours and members of the legal profession were in a conspiracy against him. Dr Noble said that Nikoloff's psychotic condition was deteriorating, but that it was treatable. He recommended Broadmoor Hospital would be the right place to send the accused man.

However the judge, Mr Justice May, said that while he appreciated the medical evidence, he was not sending Sabi Nikoloff to Broadmoor but was sentencing him to jail for life. The judge concluded by paying tribute to the courage of everyone who had helped at the siege.

Seven heroes of the siege were honoured by the Queen at a ceremony at Buckingham Palace in December 1976. Jim Galloway, Alan Christian, John Proudman, Gerald Oakley and Tom Dickman each received the Queen's Gallantry Medal. Jeno Back and Don Acton were both given the George Medal. Earlier in the year, the Queen's Commendation for Brave Conduct was awarded to John Thomas, and the same honour was awarded posthumously to Police Sgt Geordie Dawson and Leading Ambulanceman Terry Wilkinson. Terry's name is also remembered annually when the Terry Wilkinson Trophy is awarded to the year's best ambulance student in the region.

Perhaps the final words should be left to Ken Smith and Tom Atherton. Ken Smith, a former Leicestershire policeman now serving with the Royal Canadian Mounted Police, stated, 'Every day, members of the police force are faced with upholding the law in situations which place them in danger. A man may be killed or perhaps be wounded, but does that deter the next one from squaring up to a similar danger? Never! In Canada or Leicester, a policeman is still a policeman.'

Chief Ambulance Officer Tom Atherton said simply, 'The community owes a great deal to the people involved. Mr Wilkinson and the police officer did their duty without thinking of themselves.'

9

THE FOOTPATH MURDERS

THE MURDERS OF LYNDA MANN AND DAWN ASHWORTH AT
NARBOROUGH,
NOVEMBER 1983 AND JULY 1986

Many people believe that life in the country is both safer and
healthier than life in a city, and Kathleen Mann was no
exception. In 1970, following the break-up of her first marriage,
she moved from Leicester to the village of Narborough, where
she thought it would be a better environment to raise her two
young daughters, Susan and Lynda. Ten years later, Kathleen
married Eddie Eastwood and they bought a house in the village,
not far from Carlton Hayes psychiatric hospital. A year later they
had a baby daughter.

In 1983, Lynda Mann was a lively outgoing girl of 15, doing
well at Lutterworth grammar school. She was five feet three
inches tall with dark hair and eyes, and she had the usual interest
in clothes and music of a normal well-adjusted teenager. On the
evening of Monday 21st November, Lynda did a short spell of
child-minding for a neighbour from 5 pm until 6.15, then went
home for her tea.

She had expected to be baby-sitting for another neighbour
later, but found she was not needed as the lady was unwell and
therefore not going out, so instead Lynda visited her best friend
Karen. She paid Karen's mum some 'club money' for a donkey
jacket she was buying from her home shopping catalogue, and
then decided to walk over to Enderby to see another friend,
Caroline, to collect a record. This journey took about 15
minutes. At Caroline's house, the girls chatted but Lynda did not
stay long. She had left before *Coronation Street* started at half
past seven, Caroline was to recall later. As Lynda walked back
down Forest Road, a solitary figure was waiting near the junction with the Black Pad, watching her approach.

Although the *Concise Oxford Dictionary* defines a footpad as 'an unmounted highwayman', in Leicestershire a footpad is simply another word for a footpath. The Black Pad was an unlit tarmacked path that ran along the boundary of the hospital grounds.

When Eddie and Kathleen Eastwood returned home from an evening playing darts at the Dog and Gun, a worried Susan told them that Lynda had not come home yet. They were instantly alarmed; Eddie rang the police, but he soon realised that the story of a 15 year old girl staying out late did not rate a high priority. To the police, the situation was not uncommon and it meant the girl was out with a boyfriend or with a gang of friends and had forgotten the time. Kathleen and Eddie knew Lynda better than that. Eddie got in his car and drove round the village streets searching for his stepdaughter. On foot, he walked along the Black Pad in the bright frosty moonlight, paying particular attention to the side where new houses were being built. The other side, the hospital side, was fenced off with a high iron railing. He found nothing, and returned home alone.

Lynda's body was found at 7.20 am the next day by a hospital worker walking along the Black Pad. She was lying inside the hospital grounds by a copse of trees. The man spotted her through the fence, and thought at first that she was a partially clothed shop dummy. Then realising that it could be more serious than that, he ran along to the nearby gate; he found it was unlocked and hurried over to where the girl lay. She was wearing her donkey jacket and upper clothing but her jeans, tights, pants and shoes were rolled up twelve feet away. Her scarf was wound round her neck and crossed at the back. Lynda had been raped and murdered.

Eddie Eastwood was at work at Spray-Rite Ltd when he heard that a girl's body had been found near the Black Pad. He left work and rushed there immediately, but when he reached the spot he found that it had been cordoned off by the police. He told one of the policemen that he thought the victim might be his stepdaughter, Lynda. His name and details were noted and passed to Chief Superintendent David Baker. Eddie was told that the best way he could help would be to go home. As he left, he realised that he must have passed within yards of Lynda's body as he searched the area the night before. He had been concentrating his attention on the wrong side of the path.

At just after 11 am, Eddie was collected by DI Derek Pearce and taken back to the murder site, where he formally identified the body as being that of Lynda. He went home to try to comfort Kathleen and Susan. The post-mortem held on 23rd November concluded that Lynda's death was caused by 'asphyxia due to strangulation'. Soil marks on her heels and the position of her donkey jacket indicated that the body had been dragged to the spot where it was found. Laboratory analysis of the murderer's semen showed that he was a Group A secretor, a PGM 1+, a blood group shared by about 10% of English males.

The first person brought in for testing was Eddie Eastwood, who was outraged at the implication. However, from a police viewpoint, Eddie was not a blood relative of the girl, but a step-father who had been part of the family for only a few years. He had been brought up in Leicester's tough Braunstone estate, and had changed his name to Eastwood by deed poll (actually as a tribute to his favourite film star). Despite Eddie's protestation that he had been playing darts with an off-duty policeman on the Monday evening, he was taken in for the blood test. And then, of course, released. He was not in the 10% of the population that shared the killer's blood group.

A police incident room was set up in the Carlton Hayes hospital, which was somewhat ironic since at least one of the detectives expressed the strong belief that the killer would prove to be one of the patients.

One team of police officers conducted house to house enquiries in Narborough, Enderby and Littlethorpe, taking the details of all males between 13 and 34. This age range had been decided because of the high sperm count in the semen of the killer. Among the investigating officers, the frequent ribald comments about the lack of potency of those male colleagues over 34 should not be seen as a sign of callousness. They were more a way of dealing with a heartbreaking and emotionally demanding job; macho jokes to disguise the tears.

Another team checked the lists of Carlton Hayes patients going back over five years. Other teams of officers spent hundreds of hours investigating the whereabouts of men previously convicted of rape, indecent assault or 'flashing'. Although the incident

The Black Pad, Forest Road, Narborough. (David Bell)

room had computers, all the old records were hand-written and had to be laboriously typed in.

Throughout the enquiry, it was thought highly probable that the murderer, who obviously knew the network of Narborough's footpaths, must be a local man, perhaps even a teenager whom Lynda would have known.

The police also spent the next few months following up several clues that proved to be red herrings. A youth with spiky orange hair was said to have been seen with a girl in a donkey jacket that evening, but the search for him proved fruitless. A man seen running in Kipling Drive was sought. Even two boys who were seen in the village shop reading avidly about the case in the local paper were investigated.

Parents in the village met their teenage daughters off the school bus for a while. People began to speculate about their male neighbours. The parish council decided to spend £5,500 installing lights along the Black Pad. The *Leicester Mercury* printed every appeal for public assistance that the police requested. Police officers even went into local clubs and discos and asked for help from the patrons. And time went on; weeks turned into months. At the height of the investigation, 150 police officers were working on the case, falling to 50, then only eight. By the summer of 1984 there were only two. The chances of resolving the case were fading.

About five miles away from Narborough, in a laboratory at Leicester University, a research scientist named Alec Jeffreys was studying the genetic coding of the proteins that carry oxygen in the muscles. As an off-shoot of his main research, he discovered that the chromosomes that carry the whole of our genetic information have regions where the codes vary considerably from person to person. It was possible to produce a bar-code of dark bands on an X-ray film, a so-called DNA fingerprint, which is specific to every individual person. Only identical twins would have the same DNA fingerprint; everyone else would have a bar-code that was unique.

Initial interest was centred on the fact that half of a DNA fingerprint was based on that of the father, half on that of the mother. This would prove invaluable in resolving disputed paternity cases. One of the first public uses of Alec Jeffreys' discovery was in a case where the British immigration authorities were refusing to admit a Ghanaian boy who wanted to return to live in England with his mother. The Home Office were disputing whether the boy really was her son. DNA fingerprinting was used to prove the Ghanaian family's case, and the Home Office was forced to admit that their doubts about the boy's parentage were incorrect. In 1985, Alec Jeffreys was made a fellow of the Royal Society and awarded a full professorship at Leicester University.

Back in Narborough, the Eastwood family were trying to hold their lives together. In desperation, Kathleen had consulted with a spiritualist medium but had gained little comfort from her. They had also encountered a phenomenon common to many people who lose a child: friends who could not think what to say seemed to be avoiding them. Eddie, who despite suffering from arthritis had been working 90 hours a week to pay off his debts, became too depressed to work and was taken to court for obtaining credit while an undischarged bankrupt. Society seemed to be punishing the Eastwoods for being the family of a murder victim.

The Ashworths, who lived in Enderby, had no such problems. They were a happy family: Robin, a 40 year old engineer with

LEICESTERSHIRE CONSTABULARY
LET'S NOT FORGET

LYNDA MANN

Murdered a year ago in Narborough

Fifteen year old Lynda was found murdered at 7.30 a.m. on Tuesday November 22nd, 1983, in a small copse adjacent to a public footpath known locally as "The Black Pad", Forest Road, Narborough. Lynda was last seen alive at 7.30 p.m. on Monday November 21st, 1983, when she visited a friend.

Description of the deceased: 15 yrs — 5'3" — slim build — short dark coloured hair with fringe. Wearing a ¾ length black donkey jacket with wrap over front, full Dolman sleeves, large patch pockets, a standup collar, buttoned front. Mauve sweatshirt, pale blue denim jeans tapered at the ankles, and black plimsolls.

CAN YOU HELP THE POLICE WITH THEIR ENQUIRIES?

If so, contact your local police or, Wigston Police Station on Leicester 886361.

All information will be treated in the strictest of confidence.

A. Goodson
Chief Constable

A police handbill issued in 1984 on the first anniversary of the murder of Lynda Mann. (Leicestershire Constabulary)

British Gas, his wife Barbara, and two goodnatured teenage children, Dawn and Andrew. Barbara and 15 year old Dawn were more like friends than mother and daughter, often taking each other's side in family discussions. In the summer of 1986, Barbara was working three days a week at the Enderby headquarters of Next, and Dawn had a holiday job working part-time at the village newsagent's. On Thursday 31st July, she had a pleasant day at work, made even more pleasant by being given a present, a cuddly toy, by a boy who obviously liked her. It was pay day as well.

Dawn went home at half past three, and told Barbara that she was going to walk over to Narborough to have tea with her friends Sharon and Sue. Barbara asked Dawn to be back by seven o'clock as she and Robin were going to help out at the birthday party of the young son of a family friend. Dawn agreed, and set out at about four o'clock. First she nipped back to the shop where she worked to buy a pink lipstick for herself and a box of sweets for the birthday boy. Then she set off for Narborough.

She had a choice of routes; the one her parents liked her to take was on the path over the M1, then along by the motorway to King Edward Avenue. The other was down Ten Pound Lane. Ten Pound Lane, also known as Green Lane, was a grassy track with fields of hay on one side and farmland bordering Carlton Hayes hospital on the other. This way also led to King Edward Avenue, but it was both shorter and prettier than crossing the motorway. Dawn was a sensible girl, well aware of Lynda Mann's murder three years earlier on another local footpath, but that had occurred on a November evening after dark. Today was a beautiful July afternoon, so nothing bad could possibly happen. Dawn took the right fork to Ten Pound Lane and reached Narborough safely.

At Sharon Clarke's house, Dawn was told that Sharon had gone to call for Sue Allsop. At Sue's house, she heard that the two girls had gone for a walk down into the village, so Dawn decided to give up the idea of finding her friends and to walk back to Enderby. Again, she decided to go via Ten Pound Lane. She was wearing a blouse over a white polo-neck jumper, and a white flared skirt, and she was carrying her denim jacket. As with Lynda Mann three years earlier, the silent figure of a solitary man watched her approach along the footpath.

At about 5 pm, Robin Ashworth received a phone call from Sue Allsop, asking to speak to Dawn and explaining that she had been out when Dawn had called. Robin said that Dawn had not got back yet. By 7.30, Barbara and Robin were worried, but they thought it possible that Dawn had forgotten she had promised to be back by seven o'clock. In that case she would be working to her normal 'home by 9.30' schedule. They drove over to the Allsops and spoke to Sue and Sharon, then went home and waited anxiously. At 9.40 pm Robin phoned the police. Walking the village footpaths later that night, Robin was very conscious that Eddie Eastwood had done the same thing in November 1983. The frightening coincidences of Dawn's disappearance and Lynda's murder were not lost on the police; the next day, Friday 1st August, a massive police search began. The headline in Friday's *Leicester Mercury* read: 'Huge Hunt For Missing Schoolgirl', and the next day it was: 'Dawn: Fears Grow For Her Safety'.

Dawn's body, naked from the waist down, was found in bushes by Ten Pound Lane. Hay, nettles and branches had been heaped over her, hiding her from the view of passers-by. Like Lynda Mann, Dawn had been raped and strangled, though in the view of the pathologist she may have been murdered then raped afterwards.

Monday's *Mercury* headline was: 'Dawn: Hunt For A Double Killer'. It seemed obvious that the killer of both girls was the same man, a serial killer. The murder hunt intensified and involved over 200 police officers. A re-enactment of Dawn's last walk was made, with a young policewoman taking the girl's place. Dawn's parents appeared at a press conference, appealing for anyone sheltering the killer to come forward. Two anonymous local businessmen put up a reward of £15,000 for information leading to the arrest of the murderer.

Witnesses came forward again with clues: a blond man seen running near the M1 motorway; a man crouching in long grass near King Edward Avenue; a scream heard in the area at five o'clock on the Thursday afternoon; a motorcyclist with a red helmet seen near the M1 bridge.

It was this motorcyclist who began to take on a new significance. He had been seen riding his bike along Ten Pound Lane on the day in question. He was also seen riding past the

Ashworth house the day after the murder. A policewoman remembered a boy with a motorbike taking an intense interest in the search for Dawn's body.

At 5 am on Friday 8th August, the police arrested a local 17 year old youth in connection with Dawn's death. He was a kitchen porter at Carlton Hayes hospital, and he owned a motorbike and red helmet. Evidence began to emerge that the youth had a history of molesting very young girls. When the police learned that he had described the location of Dawn's body to a friend before the information had been made public, they were convinced that they had got their man.

All they needed was a confession. The youth was questioned at length at Wigston police station beginning at 8.09 am that morning. During the course of several interviews totalling 15 hours, the suspect admitted the murder, then denied it, then confessed again. Some of the details he got wrong, others were completely accurate. After breakfast on the Saturday morning, he signed a confession to the murder of Dawn Ashworth but continued to deny killing Lynda Mann three years earlier, when he would have been 14. This denial was regarded by the officers with great scepticism. The two killings were so similar that they felt he must have done both of them. The youth appeared in court on Monday 11th August charged with Dawn's murder and was remanded in police custody for three days.

Then someone remembered Professor Alec Jeffreys and his genetic fingerprinting. Scientific evidence to back up the confession would make the case watertight and could tie the two cases together. Samples of semen from both murders were sent to Leicester University, along with a blood sample from the youth under arrest. When Alec Jeffreys rang back with his findings he was able to confirm to the police that both murders were committed by the same man, as they had always assumed. However, his other piece of information was completely unexpected and it was devastating: neither killing could possibly have been done by the kitchen porter they had charged, the youth who had signed the confession, the man in custody!

Some of the police on the murder squad were dumbstruck. Others were very vocal on the subject of college professors who could overturn all their careful investigations with one scientific analysis. What hit them all was that their utter certainty that they had got the right man was destroyed.

Most people find it hard to understand why anyone who has not committed a crime would confess to one. What happens in an interview to persuade anyone to claim falsely to have murdered?

Whatever the sequence of events that led to the kitchen porter's confession, he was set free on 21st November 1986 by the court at Leicester Castle, on the recommendation of the Crown Prosecutor, Gordon Etherington. Legal history had been made. A murder suspect had been freed as a result of genetic fingerprinting.

And the police were back to square one. They had two murders, one of them three years old, and no real suspects. New leads had to be sought and old information rechecked. The local daily newspaper, the *Leicester Mercury*, published a four-page special edition on the murder, delivered free to all houses in Narborough, Enderby and Littlethorpe. The investigation was featured on *Crimewatch UK*. The anonymous donors of the reward upped it to £20,000. People wrote and phoned in their hundreds with snippets of information, adding to the pile that had been left unchecked since the police thought they had got their man. All these messages, almost 2,000 of them, had to be evaluated. One anonymous message named a 27 year old married man from Littlethorpe who might be worth checking; he had been investigated once as he had previous convictions for 'flashing', but he was not a high priority as he had moved to Littlethorpe a year after the first murder had taken place.

Some of the officers working on the case were still convinced that the kitchen porter might have found Dawn's body, then covered it over again. They spent time and effort trying to find evidence of this but found none.

Then, on the first day of 1987, a breath-taking decision was announced. All male residents of the three villages who had been between 14 and 31 at the time of the first murder in 1983 were 'invited' to give a blood and saliva sample. Also invited to participate were the patients of Carlton Hayes hospital, and every male with any connection with the area who had no alibi for the two murder dates. The numbers involved were enormous. The headline in the *Daily Mail* of 2nd January read: 'Murder Test for 2,000 Men'.

Daily Mail

FRIDAY, JANUARY 2, 1987   20p

INSIDE

BOYCOTT
WITH ENGLAND'S WINNERS DOWN UNDER
PAGE 44

BOTHA ✕
WILL HIS ELECTION WIN HIM TIME?
PAGE 6

BIG APPLE
WIN A FABULOUS TRIP TO NEW YORK
PAGE 30

WINNING AGAIN IN '87
THE BEST ROYAL PICTURE OF '86

Dramatic twist in double killer hunt

MURDER TEST FOR 2000 MEN

By AUBREY CHALMERS

A REVOLUTIONARY scientific technique is being used in a bid to trap a double sex killer.

More than 2,000 men in three villages are being asked to give specimens for 'genetic fingerprinting'. It is the first time the technique has been used on a wide scale.

Police emphasise that the tests are purely

Lynda . . . killed in 1983

Dawn . . . killed last August

voluntary. But anyone refusing to co-operate is likely to come under close scrutiny.

The man being hunted killed Dawn Ashworth and Lynda Mann, both 15, near the M1 in Leicestershire. The murders happened nearly three years apart, but scientists have used the 'genetic fingerprint' method to establish that the same man was responsible.

The system has already cleared a 17-year-old youth, who was charged with murdering Dawn last August. Richard Buckland was dramatically freed in November when the tests showed he was not involved in the 1983 murder of Lynda.

Now all the adult men living in the neighbouring ... of Enderby — where Dawn lived — Narborough ...'s home — and Littlethorpe have received ... them to attend testing centres to be opened ...

PRINCESS DIANA GETS THE RIDING HABIT AGAIN

... and she borrows the Queen's horse

NERVOUSLY, and with a word of encouragement from the Queen, Princess Diana got back in the saddle yesterday.

She rarely rides since an accident as a

The Queen on Wednesday

ten-year-old which made her lose her nerve.

Yesterday the Queen wanted Diana to feel confident, so she chose for her the same obedient and placid horse she had used the day before.

While the Queen was happy with a scarf and the hood on her riding cape for protection, the Princess wore a black riding hat for safety during the hour-long ride at Sandringham.

As the Queen, Princess Diana and Prince Edward gently cantered across the 20,000-acre estate, Prince Charles and the Duchess of York galloped off at a ...

Contemporary national press coverage. (Daily Mail/Solo)

This unprecedented procedure was dramatic in its simplicity: if genetic fingerprinting could prove someone innocent, then it could also track down the guilty man. It was stated that participation was entirely voluntary but the pressure to take part was immense. Everyone was supporting the sampling: police, elected councillors, the media and above all the residents in the community. If you were a male in the relevant age range it was not a good time to mention any reservations about your civil rights. No one, not even the policemen on the case, was exempt from unrelenting public pressure to take part in the blood and saliva sampling.

And in the small village of Littlethorpe, a man began to worry. He dare not give a blood sample, but he had received his letter from the police asking him to attend on 22nd January. Was there any way of avoiding the situation? There just might be. To buy a little time he could say the date was not convenient and get it put back a week or so. Perhaps he could then get someone to attend in his place, a workmate possibly. He would need to spin them a yarn, offer them money even. The only problem then would be that people giving a sample had to take in some identification which included a photograph. Otherwise they would have their photo taken on the spot and later an employer would be asked to confirm the identification.

By July the *Daily Mail* headline had proved an underestimate: 4,000 people had given a blood sample. It was on the 1st August that an unguarded bit of gossip in a pub led to a breakthrough. Four workmates from Hampshire's Bakery, including Ian Kelly and Jackie Foggin, were having a dinnertime drink in the Clarendon pub in Leicester. They were discussing the womanising habits of Colin Pitchfork, who also worked at the bakery, when Ian commented that Colin had persuaded him to take a blood test for him. The other man present then revealed that Colin had also asked him to take the test in his place, offering him £200 to do so, but that he had refused. Ian Kelly said that he had not been offered money, but had been given a story about Colin Pitchfork having taken the test for a friend, before being sent for in his own name. Ian also revealed that the deception involved switching photos in Colin Pitchfork's passport.

Jackie Foggin realised that they were discussing the DNA blood test relating to the Narborough murder inquiry and she

LEICESTERSHIRE CONSTABULARY

COMMUNICATIONS CENTRE
ST. JOHNS,
ENDERBY,
LEICESTER, LE9 5BX.

From the
2nd November 1986 our
telephone number will
be changed to
Leicester (0533) 530066

OUR REF.

YOUR REF.

Dear Sir,

You will be aware by now that a large scale Police enquiry is taking
place in this area to trace the person responsible for the tragic deaths
of two local girls, Lynda Mann aged 15 years and Dawn Ashworth, 15 years.
The success of this operation can only be achieved by the whole hearted
assistance and co-operation of the community and it is to this end we
are making a direct approach to you.

For elimination purposes we are endeavouring to obtain certain samples
from the male population of the area. These samples will consist of
blood and saliva only.

The samples will be obtained by fully qualified Medical practitioners and
when the examination of the samples has been completed, they will be
destroyed. The taking of the samples will comply with the strictest
medical standards.

THE GIVING OF SAMPLES IS COMPLETELY VOLUNTARY

Your co-operation in this matter is sought, therefore, you are invited
to attend the Blaby Rural District Council Offices, Narborough/Danemill
School, Mill Lane, Enderby between 7.00pm and 8.30 pm on

...... Thursday .... the ...22nd January...

It would be helpful if you could be in possession of some form of
identification in addition to this letter when attending.

If you are under 17 years of age, you must be accompanied by your parent
or guardian.

If you are unable to attend on the date indicated, please telephone
Leicester 482405 (Inspector THOMAS) when an alternative date will be
arranged.

Thank you for your assistance.

A. Painter

A. PAINTER - Detective Superintendent

An invitation to Colin Pitchfork to implicate himself in the murders.
(Leicestershire Constabulary)

became very disturbed. However, the idea that Colin Pitchfork could be the double killer seemed absurd and she was told to forget about it. That was easier said than done, and Jackie was unable to dismiss it from her conscience. She needed to tell someone. Over the next few weeks she looked out for the policeman son of the Clarendon publican, but failed to see him. It was Friday 18th September before she rang the police incident room in Enderby and reported the conversation she had heard in the pub six weeks earlier.

The next day, Saturday 19th September, Ian Kelly was arrested and questioned. A few hours later, Detective Inspector Michael Thomas led a team of six officers to the home of Colin Pitchfork in Littlethorpe. Pitchfork made no attempt to deny the murders and he was arrested at 5.45 pm. Talking to DI Thomas and DS Mick Mason, Pitchfork spoke at length about his childhood in Newbold Verdon and his time in the Scouts where he became a Scout leader at the age of 15, though he was thrown out after he was caught flashing. He later joined a different group as a Venture Scout, and undertook voluntary work at a Barnado's children's home, where he met the woman who was to become his wife. He admitted that he had always had the urge to expose himself to women and girls.

Questioned about the Lynda Mann murder, he said that he had dropped his wife off at her evening class, then driven his car to Narborough with his baby son in the child seat. His original plan was to find a lone girl and flash at her, but when Lynda saw him on Forest Road she had run away into the Black Pad. To the disgust of the policemen, Pitchfork was saying that it was Lynda's fault because she had not screamed or run along the road. He said that he had raped her and then had to kill her because she could have described him. On the occasion of the second killing, he had again begun with the intention of just exposing himself. As before, he claimed that the rape and murder were the victim's fault for backing away in the wrong direction, towards a farm gate which somehow 'opened itself'.

Pitchfork's attempt to blame the victims was not the only thing that shocked his questioners. Throughout the interviews he was cool and calm, showing no remorse, no feelings of any kind. He appeared to have no compunction about talking about what he had done, telling the police of two other occasions when he had

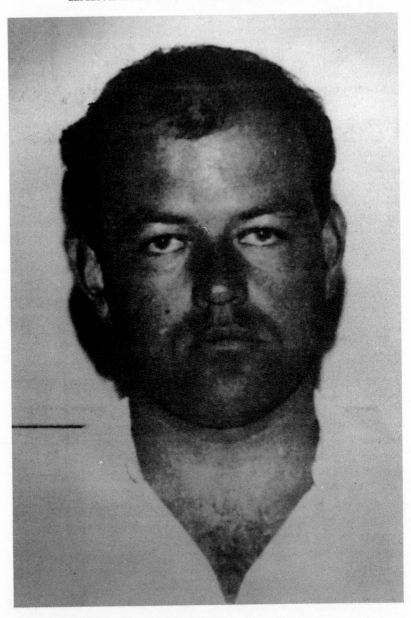

Colin Pitchfork. (Leicester Mercury)

committed sexual assaults. He seemed unable to understand what any of his victims must have felt; he had no sense of empathy at all. After the first killing, he had gone home to wash and shave, then driven to meet his wife from college. After the second, he had gone home and baked a cake.

At his trial before High Court Judge Mr Justice Otton at the Crown Court in Leicester in January 1988, Pitchfork pleaded guilty and described all his actions in a detached manner, showing no emotion. He was given two life sentences for the murders, two ten year sentences for the rapes, and two three year sentences for other sexual assaults that had taken place in 1979 and 1985, all to run concurrently. He received a further three years for the conspiracy with Ian Kelly to pervert the course of justice. Kelly was given an 18 months suspended sentence, the judge adding, 'I just about believe you did it because you accepted the story put forward by Pitchfork.'

During the trial, Colin Pitchfork was described by a Broadmoor psychiatrist as 'a psychopath of a psycho-sexual type'. Psychopaths have been described as superficially adequate, possessing initial charm which may mask deviant and unfeeling actions. They show no signs of anxiety or distress, show no shame or remorse at harmful acts. Although they can parrot ethical behaviour and repeat verbal statements of regret, it is void of meaning for them. Psychopath certainly seems the right term to describe Colin Pitchfork.

During the trial, the judge praised Professor Alec Jeffreys' discovery of DNA genetic fingerprinting, which led to Pitchfork's arrest. It is ironic to reflect that it was actually the killer's fear of genetic fingerprinting which eventually unmasked him, rather than the scientific process itself.

10

THE KLA EXECUTION

THE MURDER OF RAVINDRA MHATRE AT SAPCOTE, FEBRUARY 1984

K ashmir is one of the most beautiful places in the world, a high valley of forests and lakes, surrounded by snow-capped mountains. The Mughal emperors described it simply as Paradise. Located in the Himalayan mountains of northern India, Kashmir has common borders with both Pakistan and China, making it a very strategic and politically sensitive area.

It is also a politically contentious land. When India was partitioned in 1947, the Maharajah of Kashmir – a Hindu – opted to join India rather than Pakistan, despite the fact that three-quarters of Kashmiris were Muslim. Pakistan has always claimed Kashmir as its own. The people of Kashmir are split three ways on the issue: some wishing to be part of Pakistan, others preferring to remain part of India, and a substantial group wanting to achieve an independent Kashmir. The politics of the area are complex and continually developing, with small radical groups splitting off from their more orthodox parent bodies.

The turbulent politics of this Himalayan valley came to Leicestershire in February 1984 when the body of Ravindra Mhatre, an Indian diplomat, was found on an isolated farm track in the south-east of the county.

Red Hill Farm, near the village of Sapcote, belonged to brothers Arthur and Roy Tallis who worked the 100 acre dairy farm together. Roy travelled in from his home in Hinckley every day, but Arthur lived in the farmhouse with his wife, Joyce. On the evening of Sunday 5th February, Arthur and Joyce had been visiting friends in Stoney Stanton, returning home at about 10 pm. They turned into the driveway of the farm and had driven about 40 yards when the car headlights picked out an object on the ground. At first it looked like a bundle of rags, lying to the left of the drive. They stopped the car and Arthur went up to it. 'When I was a few yards away, I could see it was a body,' he said. 'There was blood around the face and nose. At first I thought the man had been in a fight, not realising that he was dead. I got back into the car and drove straight to the police station in Hinckley.'

PC Malcolm Benn was the first policeman on the scene; he noted that the body was lying on its back with its feet towards the road, the left arm outstretched and clutching a black woollen hat. The dead man was wearing a grey suit, white shirt, and a black coat with a fur collar. There was a cloth tied around his head. PC Benn radioed his station, and the scene was soon busy with police activity. When Dr Victor Pugh, the consultant pathologist from Leicester Royal Infirmary, arrived on the scene he made a preliminary examination of the body, finding that the man had been shot in the head and body at point blank range. It was not clear at this stage whether the man had been killed at the spot, or killed elsewhere and his body dumped at the farm. However, forensic investigation of the spot confirmed that the man had indeed been shot in the driveway of Red Hill Farm.

The body was soon identified as that of 48 year old Ravindra Mhatre, the Assistant High Commissioner based at the Indian High Commission in Birmingham. Mr Mhatre had disappeared on his way home from work on the previous Friday. A witness had seen the missing man being bundled into a red four-door saloon car – thought to be a Ford Escort – by three Asian men, close to the diplomat's home in the Bartley Green area of Birmingham. Reuters News Agency in Fleet Street had received a hand-delivered letter from the previously unknown Kashmir Liberation Army, demanding that the Indian government release several Kashmiri political prisoners being held in Indian gaols, including Maqbool Butt who was under sentence of death. The letter also demanded a ransom of £1,000,000.

From this point the inquiry was conducted jointly by detectives from Leicestershire and the West Midlands, assisted by officers from Scotland Yard. In Birmingham members of the West Midlands police went to Mr Mhatre's home to break the news of the diplomat's death to Mrs Shobia Mhatre and her 14 year old daughter Asha. The London based Indian High Commissioner, Dr Seyid Mohammed, whose term of office in Britain had been due to end that very week, deferred his return to India. He cancelled all his public engagements and travelled to Birmingham to offer his sympathy and to bring what comfort he could to Ravindra Mhatre's widow and daughter.

An incident room was set up in the Charles Street police station in Leicester, and back in the village of Sapcote the officer in charge of the scene of crime, Detective Inspector Alan Ottey, instigated a search of the immediate area of Red Hill Farm. This search paid off when a balaclava style ski-mask was discovered. Scientific examination led detectives to conclude that the ski-mask, bearing a Wynnster label, did belong to one of the killers. Stockists in Leicester and other parts of the Midlands were questioned to see if they had sold one of the masks recently, particularly to a male Asian customer.

In India, the prime minister, Mrs Indira Gandhi, called in her top Cabinet for an emergency meeting. She ordered an immediate tightening of security at Indian offices throughout the world, and a senior Indian police officer was sent to Britain to help with the investigation.

In Leicester, community leaders were determined that the murder should not damage the good relationship between the various peoples of the city. Greville Janner, the MP for West Leicester and a personal friend of the Gandhi family, sent a message to Mrs Gandhi expressing deepest condolences at the murder. Mr Liaquat Hussain, secretary-general of the All Jamu and Kashmir Muslim Conference, said that although his organisation campaigned for the right of the Kashmiri people to self-determination, they worked in a peaceful manner, and 'would never support this sort of violence.' Mohammed Yagub Khan, deputy secretary of the same group, said that his group were prepared to help the police in any way.

Pravin Lukka, the East Midlands secretary of the Confederation of Indian Organisations, stated: 'This murder was a disgraceful and cowardly act that must be condemned by everyone. People from the sub-continent now living here must realise that they cannot influence the governments of India, Pakistan, Bangladesh, or anywhere - they cannot even vote there now. Kashmir is a long-running problem between India and Pakistan. I hope that it will soon be solved, but to murder innocent diplomats in this cowardly way will achieve nothing.'

Ratilal Ganatra, president of the Federation of Indian Organisations, said, 'The social harmony and good race relations of Leicester must not be harmed by this terrible act. People should react calmly. Britain has a very good police force and legal system, and it must be left to them to find the killers.'

This unanimity of reaction to the crime was dented a week after the murder, when Maqbool Butt was hanged in Delhi. He was the Kashmiri man whose release had been demanded by the KLA when they kidnapped Ravindra Mhatre, and had been found guilty of murder by an Indian court eight years earlier. The fact that he was executed just a week after the killing of Ravindra Mhatre led many Kashmiris to see it as an act of revenge by the Indian government. Mohammed Jahangir Mir of the Leicester-based Kashmir League Party said that he was 'deeply disappointed' with the Indian government's action. Mohammed Yagub Khan of the All Jamu and Kashmir Muslim Conference said, 'We condemn violence, but this action will only make things worse.'

However, Leicester's Asian community closed ranks once more on 26th February, when a memorial service was held at Belgrave Neighbourhood Centre. The service was organized by Councillor Krishan Khanna and Ratilal Ganatra, and it was attended by Hindus, Muslims, Sikhs and Jains who joined together to pay tribute to the murdered man. Although Ravindra Mhatre had been based in Birmingham, his work covered the whole of the Midlands and he was well known and very well respected in Leicester. Leicestershire's Assistant Chief Constable, Brian Pollard described the diplomat as a gentle, quiet family man who had spent his life in the service of others. Ratilal Ganatra added that he was a very humble, intelligent man well-known for his humanity and goodwill. Councillor Yusef Chaudary said, 'I am pleased to see that in spite of what has happened, we have maintained our unity, and that unity will bring whoever has committed this brutal murder to justice.'

Meanwhile the police investigations were continuing. Having established that Ravindra Mhatre had been killed at the place where he was found, one line of enquiry was into where he had been kept between his kidnapping on Friday evening and the discovery of his body on Sunday night. It was thought possible that he had been held in Leicester and then brought to Sapcote along the M69. The murder location was less than two miles from Junction 2 of that motorway.

On Sunday 12th February, the police set up checkpoints on the roads around Sapcote, asking motorists whether they had driven on the A5070 or the B4069 on the previous Sunday between 8 pm and 10 pm, and if so, whether they had seen any parked cars or indeed anything at all that might be of help in the murder hunt.

The murder squad were also searching for Ravindra Mhatre's missing heavy-rimmed spectacles, his leather gloves, his blue striped tie and a lunchbox he was thought to be carrying at the time of his abduction. One item that did turn up was the diplomat's West Midlands travel card, found two days after the murder by a BR employee near the track at Toton in Nottinghamshire. Police believed that it had been thrown from a train and concluded that one of the kidnappers must have been travelling north by rail on the main London–Sheffield line.

The woman who had witnessed the kidnapping in Birmingham was able to give a good description of the driver of the red car involved. He was described as a dark-skinned man between 30 and 40, with a moustache and collar-length hair with a centre parting. She said that there were three other men in the car.

The police continued to look into the Kashmir Liberation Army; this was a new name among Kashmiri political groups, but it was thought that it was likely to be a splinter group that had split off from the long-established Kashmir Liberation Front. Officers of the KLF stated that they knew nothing of the breakaway KLA. However, detectives managed to obtain tapes of telephone calls made by self-proclaimed members of the KLA to Abdul Ansari, a member of the KLF. The detectives working on the case listened to these tapes with considerable interest.

By the end of February, four men had been arrested in connection with the kidnapping and unlawful imprisonment of Ravindra Mhatre. By May, this had grown to five, with two of them also charged with the murder. All five were remanded in custody, with a sixth man – who faced a lesser charge – released on bail. The two charged with killing the diplomat were 22 year old Mohammed Riaz, a Business Studies student at Leicester Polytechnic, and 27 year old Abdul Raja, a student in Paris.

The three facing kidnapping and false imprisonment charges were Mohammed Bhatti, Janghir Mirza and Abdul Ansari, all residents of Birmingham and members of the KLF. The sixth man, Mohammed Ishaq of Luton, who was not a member of the KLF, was charged with trying to obtain a false passport for Raja. All the men denied the charges.

The trial of the six men opened on 14th January 1985. Mr Ivor Judge QC, prosecuting, said that Ravindra Mhatre had been shot at point blank range in a lonely Leicester lane by political extremists, who had chosen their victim at random to use him as a convenient pawn. They had kidnapped Mr Mhatre in Birmingham, held him at a secret address, and finally executed him in cold blood. He had been selected because he was a member of India's diplomatic service, in order to bring pressure on the Indian government. He had only once been to Kashmir and that was for a holiday. He died as a victim of international terrorism caused by problems thousands of miles away. The dead man had no enemies; he had died simply because of his job.

Six days into the trial, all the accused men changed their pleas. Mohammed Bhatti (43) admitted the charge of kidnapping. Bhatti, Mirza and Ansari all admitted concealing and disposing of evidence. The Luton man, Mohammed Ishaq, admitted making a false statement to obtain a passport. Mr Ivor Judge QC said that the pleas were acceptable to the prosecution and the four men were remanded in custody to be sentenced at the end of the trial against Riaz and Raja.

Shortly after this, Riaz and Raja admitted holding Ravindra Mhatre at a secret address in Birmingham but continued to plead not guilty to his murder. Their trial continued.

Abdul Raja alleged to the jury that he had been beaten up by two police officers on a journey from Holyhead to the West Midlands. He said that after he had been arrested in Holyhead while attempting to leave the country, the two detectives had hit him, pulled his hair and sworn at him while he was being driven back to Birmingham. This was why he had refused to co-operate with them or make a statement. He now wished to tell the truth. He stated that when he agreed to take part in the operation he had no idea that Mr Mhatre was going to be killed. He claimed that he was horrified when the diplomat was shot in front of him.

Mohammed Riaz, of Jarrom Street, Leicester, told the jury that he had never intended that the diplomat should be shot. Riaz claimed that he was under a great deal of pressure from the

Kashmiri community at large to take part. He said that he had been driven from Leicester to Birmingham by a member of the KLA, Mushrat Iqbal, who told him that he would have to look after Mr Mhatre while he negotiated with the Indian authorities for the release of political prisoners being held in Kashmir. He admitted holding Mr Mhatre prisoner at a secret address, adding that, 'We knew we were not going to get any hassle from him because we knew he was ill.' Two days later, he was told that the kidnapped diplomat was going to be shot. He travelled in the car that drove Ravindra Mhatre to Sapcote. Also in the car were his brother, another man and Abdul Raja. Riaz claimed that he and his brother remained in the car while the other men got out. They turned the car round, and when they returned to pick up the others, they found that only Raja and the other man were waiting. They looked shaken and panicky, and said that they had killed Mhatre.

The trial lasted for 16 days and at the end of it the jury found both men, Mohammed Riaz and Abdul Raja, guilty of murder by an 11–1 majority verdict. Both were given life sentences. Mohammed Bhatti received a 20 year sentence for kidnapping and for concealing evidence knowing a murder had been committed. Mirza and Ansari, who admitted assisting the offenders, were given three and two years respectively. Mohammed Ishaq was fined £500 for making a false statement to obtain a false passport for Raja.

No other men were brought to court in this case. Attempts by Leon Brittan, the Home Secretary, to have three other men – Mohammed Iqbal, Azhar Mahmood and Mohammed Mirzen – extradited from Pakistan proved unfruitful.

11

A DARK SECRET

THE MURDERS OF CAROLINE OSBORNE AND AMANDA
WEEDON AT LEICESTER,
JULY 1983 AND APRIL 1985

C aroline Osborne was a 33 year old pet beautician with her
own business, an animal grooming parlour called Clippapet.
Although she was separated from her musician husband Gary, it
was by mutual agreement and she still got on well with him. She
had no steady boyfriend but had several male friends that she
saw socially. She enjoyed her work, she had a full social life, and
her future seemed bright. On the evening of Friday 29th July
1983, she went to an area known as Aylestone Meadows to take
two dogs for a walk. One was her own black labrador and the
other a crossbred brindle retriever belonging to her neighbour.
Both dogs were called Tammy. Caroline's other dog, a fiercely
protective alsatian called Gemma, usually went with them but on
this occasion Gemma was lame and had to be left at home.

Later that evening, the black labrador returned alone to Caroline's home at her Clippapet business premises in Danvers
Road, Leicester. Neighbours heard the dog howling and, realising
something was wrong, called out the police. A search was made
of the area of thick undergrowth and leafy towpaths close to the
river Soar, but nothing was found that night.

The search was resumed on the Saturday morning, and at
10.30 am a police dog handler, PC David Warsop, was walking
down a path leading to Pebble Beach when his dog raised its
head and ran across an area of burnt-out grass. PC Warsop followed and found Caroline's body in long grass 15 feet down an
embankment. Tammy, the brindle retriever, was guarding the
body and would not let the policeman or his dog approach it.
Tammy's owner was fetched from her home, and the dog came
to her immediately. The police were now able to examine the

99

body. They found that Caroline had been stabbed to death. Her body was fully clothed but her feet and ankles were bound together. She had not been sexually assaulted or robbed.

The police murder squad led by Detective Superintendent Alan Stagg began its investigations. Swabs were taken from both dogs, in the hope of finding particles of clothing or blood specks. A large area around the river was sealed off and an inch by inch search of the undergrowth began, while frogmen searched the river itself. House to house enquiries were made in the streets to the north and west of Aylestone Meadows. John Douglas of Wolverton Road was able to tell them that he had seen the black labrador, wet through and walking up and down the canal bank. He had told it to go home and it had run off. This was three hours before the dog had turned up howling in Danvers Road.

Dr Roger Mugford, a psychologist with degrees in animal behaviour from Hull University and the University of Pennsylvania, said that the dogs had acted in co-operative and intelligent teamwork after the attack. He described the labrador and retriever as highly evolved social animals. 'It is quite consistent for there to be an understanding between them – that one dog should stay with its master or mistress and the other should go for help.' Dr Mugford thought it likely that Caroline Osborne had known her killer.

At a press conference, Alan Stagg stated, 'This is a serious incident: this killer could strike again. Women and girls should not go out into lonely spots on their own.' Aylestone Meadows, an area lying between the Grand Union Canal section of the river Soar and the river Biam, contains a sportsground belonging to Emgas and a nature sanctuary. It is very popular with families and courting couples, any of whom might have seen something significant. Alan Stagg called on anyone out on Aylestone Meadows on the Friday evening to come forward, particularly if they had seen the auburn haired Caroline Osborne, who was wearing a red and white halter-neck teeshirt, faded blue jeans and blue trainers, or a black dog wandering loose. The police were keen to talk to an Asian family of two adults and three small children who were seen walking the paths, and also four children playing near an electricity pylon who had been spoken to by a uniformed river warden. Many people did come forward. In all, the police managed to interview nearly 300 people who

The gas holder on Aylestone Meadows. (David Bell)

were in the area on the night of the murder, as well as all the customers of Clippapet.

People came forward to talk about Caroline Osborne too, describing her as a sensitive and kind animal lover. Mrs Mary Tuckey of Quorn, who owned the Whitehouse kennels in Coalville where Caroline first started working, said 'It is a terrible tragedy because she was such a kind person. She was a quiet girl but extremely loving. She stayed with us for nine months and was a great help to me because my husband was ill.' Mrs Marion Lovelace of the Groomers Association, who had called on Caroline a few days before her death, said, 'I was impressed by her. She was kind and sympathetic.' Others told how she would undercharge elderly customers, and transport their dogs free of charge to and from the shop. A senior police officer on the case said that Caroline was an honest, decent, industrious young woman, adding, 'This makes the crime all the more wicked and baffling.'

The investigators did discover a silver necklace with a heart shaped pendant close to the scene, and also the wooden handle of a kitchen knife though there was no indication that it was from the murder weapon. Despite the large number of people interviewed, the police found no one who had seen Caroline Osborne walking her dogs on the Friday evening. The police were anxious to talk to a number of individuals. One was a man of about 30, about five feet ten inches tall, who was observed near the murder spot earlier in the day. He was unshaven, had dark brown collar-length hair and was wearing a black polo-neck jumper, a long sleeved sweater and dark trousers with a pair of gloves hanging out of his back pocket. The police thought that his attire was rather surprising in view of the temperature of 80°F on July 29th. Another man sought was known to have met Caroline on several occasions; he was five feet eight inches, with dark wavy hair and said to be clean shaven and goodlooking. A third man sought was a tall youth of about 16 seen sitting on a bridge at Pebble Beach, throwing stones into the water.

At the inquest into Caroline's death, pathologist Dr Clive Bouch revealed that she had been stabbed ten times in the neck, arms and chest. There were no signs that she had put up a struggle, and the chest wounds were likely to have been inflicted while she was standing. He said that tests on the ligatures binding her ankles indicated that she may have been tied up after her death.

The coroner, Mr Michael Chapman, recorded a verdict of unlawful killing, adding, 'It almost certainly must have been someone she knew who killed her.'

The police investigations continued for months. A year after the murder the scene was reconstructed on BBC's *Crimewatch*. Although the BBC received 30 calls and Wigston police station another 50 following the television broadcast, the leads they gave all petered out.

A seemingly separate murder occurred shortly after four o'clock on the afternoon of Saturday 27th April 1985, when a young nurse was stabbed to death on a footpath near Groby Road hospital. This was in a completely different area of Leicester from the Aylestone Meadows killing. Amanda Weedon had spent her lunchtime shopping in Leicester with her fiance, Clifford Eversfield. The couple were excited as they were to collect the keys to their new house in two days time. In the early afternoon, Clifford left for Whetstone to watch the football team of which he was the manager. Amanda went to a friend's house on

Chantry Lane, near the Groby Road hospital. (David Bell)

the Beaumont Leys estate, before setting off for the hospital at 3.45 pm. Part of her journey took her along a footpath known as Chantry Lane running between Groby Road hospital and Gilroes cemetery.

The body of 21 year old Amanda was discovered by a teenage girl at 4.15 pm in a hedgerow on the lonely tree-lined footpath, close to a large redbrick house called The Chantry, a halfway house for psychiatric patients. Dr Kyee Htay Han was called out from the hospital and tried to revive the girl, but in vain. Amanda had been stabbed 37 times in the neck, chest and thigh. She had not been sexually assaulted. Her handbag containing a small amount of money and a bank cashcard was missing, though the bankcard was later discovered in Gilroes cemetery.

The police soon revealed that both Chantry Lane and Gilroes cemetery were the haunts of unsavoury characters, the footpath being a favourite spot for 'flashers' and the cemetery being used by young glue-sniffers. The police also commented that they had not ruled out a possible connection with the unsolved murders of Lynda Mann, the schoolgirl raped and strangled in November 1983 on a footpath near the grounds of another hospital, and of

LEICESTERSHIRE CONSTABULARY

MURDER

Of Caroline Osborne (nee Smith). Proprietor of 'Clippapet', 107 Danvers Road, Leicester, on 29th July, 1983, whilst walking two dogs on the Aylestone Meadows, Leicester.

Do you recall seeing Caroline at any time in company with a man, two of whom have been described as follows:—

1st Man (Photo-fit impression)

1st Man (Photo-fit impression)

35-36 years, approx 6 feet tall, average build, English but olive skinned, dark wavy hair, small moustache. Casual clothing. On occasions wore silver coloured square digital watch, silver bracelet and silver medallion on chain around neck. Known to frequent Public Houses in Leicester.

2nd Man

Approx 35 years, 5'8" – 9" tall, average build, athletic stature, fair hair neat, ears visible. Casual Clothing.
In possession of small van, dark blue colour with white lettering on sides.

If you think you know these men or any other associates of Caroline please contact the Police Murder Incident Room at Wigston, telephone number: 813121 or any Police Station.

A REWARD OF £4,000 IS OFFERED FOR INFORMATION LEADING TO THE ARREST AND SUBSEQUENT CONVICTION OF THE MURDERER.

Caroline Osborne stabbed to death on Aylestone Meadows in July 1983.

At a press conference, Detective Chief Superintendent David Baker appealed for anyone who had seen a man, possibly blood-stained and carrying a knife, to come forward. A member of staff from The Chantry reported looking through a window and seeing a shadowy figure lurking about the footpath at about four o'clock.

The following day, the police issued a description of a man they wanted to interview. He was a very tall man, wearing dark-coloured clothing, probably khaki or olive green, who had been seen at 4.05 pm a few yards from the murder spot. David Baker stated, 'If anyone has seen this man they should get in touch with us urgently. If he was legitimately walking down the footpath, he should come forward and be eliminated from the enquiry.'

Mrs Olive Weir who lived on the Beaumont Leys estate thought the description sounded rather like her 18 year old grandson Paul, who used her garage as a fitness studio. She urged Paul to go to the police and clear his name, and eventually he did so. From the moment Paul Bostock walked into Blackbird Road police station, the solution to two savage murders that had shocked the Leicester community began to draw nearer. As detectives questioned Bostock, they became more and more suspicious of his story. When police officers went to search his home on Blakesly Walk, what they found there convinced them that they had discovered the killer of both Amanda Weedon and Caroline Osborne. As well as posters and drawings of ritual tortures and murders, they found a collection of knives and martial arts weapons, and a 1984 diary with the give-away phrase 'Anniversary 1 year' written on the page for 28th/29th July, exactly a year after Caroline Osborne's death.

Paul Bostock, six feet five inches in height and weighing 15 stones, was charged with both murders. At his trial in June 1986 it emerged that in 1983 Paul had been living in Walton Street, four streets away from Caroline Osborne, and that his family's dogs had been groomed at Clippapet. Paul had in fact been interviewed in connection with the Caroline Osborne murder several times, but his alibi that he was home on 29th July had been accepted.

Mr David Farrar QC, the prosecuting counsel, said that

A tell-tale page from Bostock's diary. (Leicester Mercury)

A Leicester Mercury reporter revisits the crime scene where Amanda Weedon was murdered. (Leicester Mercury)

Bostock was a sexual sadist with an unhealthy fascination for knives, the occult and black magic. He stated that Bostock was just 16 when he murdered Caroline Osborne, tying her hands and feet before goading her, then stabbing her to death. Two years later, moments after visiting Caroline's grave in Gilroes cemetery, he attacked nurse Amanda Weedon on a footpath near the hospital where she worked. There was evidence that he had taunted Amanda too before viciously stabbing her more than 30 times. Bostock had told the police that he had approached Amanda Weedon, and attacked her when she rebuffed him, but that he could not remember either murder clearly. He was seen by a number of people as he disposed of his knife in Gilroes cemetery, near the murder scene.

The defending counsel, Mr Anthony Smith QC, told the court that Paul Bostock had written several letters to a girl he had met at the seaside in 1983. To her he was always gentleness and kind-

Paul Bostock. (Neville Chadwick Photographic Agency, Leicester)

ness itself. After his arrest for the two murders, he wrote to her, 'I have ruined my victims' families' lives, my family's life, and the life I had planned for us together. I cannot look my parents in the eye, I cannot look you in the eye, I cannot face myself and I can hardly look at the detectives.'

Passing sentence, the judge, Mr Justice Tucker, said that Bostock was a very dangerous young man. He would be sentenced to life imprisonment for the murder of Amanda Weedon, and would be detained during Her Majesty's pleasure for the earlier murder of Caroline Osborne.

Comments from everyone who had known Paul Bostock were unanimous; he was polite and gentle! Colin Underwood who had trained him in karate said, 'He was polite and placid. Sometimes people lose their temper if someone accidentally hurts them, but Paul would not. He was always in control of himself.' His former headmaster described him as a nice boy and a popular, conscientious worker, adding, 'He is the most unlikely character to have been involved in anything like this.' His coach at West Leicester Rugby Union youth team said, 'He dislikes aggression and violence and it was very difficult to get some fire into his belly.' Neighbours of the Bostock family and Paul Bostock's workmates all used one phrase to describe the man they knew: 'He was a gentle giant.'

But Paul Bostock was a gentle giant with a dark side to his personality. According to one of the detectives on the case, 'He is very dangerous and completely unstable. If he was still on the loose, I am sure we would be searching for another Yorkshire Ripper.'

12

A LOOPHOLE
IN THE LAW

THE KILLING OF SUSAN RUDMAN AT BIRSTALL,
NOVEMBER 1991

T he marriage of Susan and Jim Rudman began to deteriorate
after the birth of their second child, James, in July 1991. In
October, 41 year old Susan left her home, taking her three year
old daughter Alexandra and baby James with her. She began
divorce proceedings and attempted to have her husband legally
ousted from the family home. However, on 29th October, a
County Court judge refused her request and advised her to return
to the matrimonial home. The following day, a County Court
order was made forbidding Jim Rudman from assaulting, molesting or interfering with his wife. Susan Rudman returned to her
home in the village of Birstall on 1st November but the argument
that broke out between Susan and James three days later led
directly to Susan's death. The furious confrontation took place in
the kitchen of their Loughborough Road home, and Susan was
knocked to the floor, then stabbed 20 times.

After the stabbing, James Rudman drove his severely injured
wife to the Leicester Royal Infirmary, but dropped her outside.
There she was noticed by two passers-by who realised the ser-
iousness of her condition and informed the hospital receptionist.
Susan Rudman was rushed to the operating theatre but surgeons
were unable to save her life.

The police soon picked up Jim Rudman, a 32 year old self-
employed computer engineer. He was taken to Syston police
station where he was charged with the murder of his wife.

During Rudman's trial in August 1992, he admitted killing his
wife but claimed diminished responsibility on the grounds of
depression and mental illness. He gave evidence that during the
furious row that led to Susan's death, she had been saying
'wicked things' to him and had smashed his computer unit to the

ground. He remembered being angry and knocking her down, but could not recall picking up a knife. When he realised she had been stabbed, he had taken her to hospital.

The defence counsel, Jonathan Goldberg, said that five medical experts had agreed that James Rudman was mentally ill. While on remand at a psychiatric hospital he had tried to kill himself three times, once an attempted self-electrocution. Stephen Coward QC, the prosecuting counsel, accepted that Rudman was mentally ill with depression when he killed his wife.

The judge, Mr Justice McCullough, said that Rudman's illness was a reactive depression, reactive to the state of affairs which he had himself brought about. Therefore James Rudman was still responsible for his actions, even though that responsibility was diminished. The judge said that his initial intention had been to sentence Rudman to a five year term in prison, but that, in view of the evidence that the defendant would not be well enough to be released for at least 18 months, he was imposing a hospital order under Section 37 of the Mental Health Act 1983.

So far, the story has been a tragic one of mental illness and marriage breakdown, leading to a violent death: devastating for those involved, but in no way unusual. What occurred a year after the trial made the case of national concern with international ramifications. James Rudman was sent to Arnold Lodge, a secure unit within Leicester's Towers Hospital, but on 1st August 1993 James walked out of the grounds while on unaccompanied parole, and left the Leicester area. The initial local reaction of irritation that someone who had killed had been allowed to 'escape' soon turned to incredulity.

When people learned that if Rudman managed to avoid detection for a month, then he would have regained his freedom permanently, they were amazed and shocked. But that was the law: if he was not caught within 28 days, he would have proved that he was able to look after himself and he could not be forced back into hospital. The family of his dead wife were hurt and angry. Susan's mother, Kathleen, stated, 'If a man kills and is put away so long and then just walks out, then there is no justice. They should change the law.' Susan's brother, Steve Thornton, agreed: 'The situation is farcical. This is the last thing my mother needs. She is trying to lead as normal a life as possible but she is still feeling grief.' Steve, who had known Jim Rudman since their schooldays, said that in view of the crime he had committed, his brother-in-law should have been supervised at all times, especially when walking in the hospital grounds.

A different view was expressed by Dr James Earp, director of Trent Regional Forensic Service, who stressed that it would be impossible to rehabilitate patients and reintroduce them into the community if they were constantly locked up. Stuart Calder, a UNISON spokesman at Arnold Lodge, stated, 'We want to make people aware that we are a hospital, which is not something generally accepted when we are talking about nursing people who have committed some form of offence against society. Every individual is regularly assessed as to their level of dangerousness.' He did however agree with Steve Thornton on one thing: 'I do not think any of us would dispute the fact that the law needs to be looked at.'

Meanwhile the police were trying to find the missing man before the 28 days ran out. DI Mick Creedon said, 'I am convinced that on day 29, he could turn up smiling.' Reported sightings of James Rudman around Leicestershire were checked out, but all proved fruitless. A week passed, then another. Detectives began to investigate the possibility that he had fled abroad to wait out the 28 day period. A third week passed. A team of officers from Syston police station began to liaise with the Garda Siochana in Ireland. Even when 26, then 27, days had expired, the tenacious team of detectives did not give up, though they must have begun to privately despair of finding the fugitive in time.

On the 28th day, one hour before the deadline, the Garda found Rudman staying at a relative's house near Tralee. He was taken into custody and remanded to Cork prison. He had been caught just 62 minutes before the 28 day period expired! Back in Leicester, the family of Susan Rudman expressed their relief. 'I think we will all sleep easier,' said Steve Thornton.

James Rudman appeared in court at Tralee on 1st September and an extradition order was granted. The missing man was taken to Dublin airport and flown back to England, to be returned to Arnold Lodge. Although the Thornton family were pleased with the outcome, they expressed their intention to continue with a campaign to seal the 28 days loophole in the law.

Seven thousand signatures were collected on a petition to amend the Mental Health Act.

In December 1993, Keith Vaz, the Member of Parliament for Leicester East, stated, 'This is a very important petition. It is the best way we have of keeping the whole issue alive. The Government has spent three months in consultations between the Home Office, the Lord Chancellor's department and the Health department in trying to re-frame the law. This petition will be a very important boost to remind ministers that there is a groundswell of opinion that this law should be changed.'

Steve Thornton agreed, adding, 'Nobody should be put through what we've had to go through.'

13

THE JEALOUS SON

THE MURDER OF DEREK AND EILEEN SEVERS AT UPPER
HAMBLETON, NOVEMBER 1993

When Derek and Eileen Severs went missing in November 1993 it was not their 37 year old son who reported their absence to the police, but worried friends and neighbours. Derek and Eileen lived in an attractive £300,000 bungalow in the picturesque village of Upper Hambleton which, since the creation of Rutland Water in 1975, is now situated on a peninsula in the middle of the lake.

Both were in their late sixties. Derek Severs, a retired ICI executive, took life gently and enjoyed his retirement. Eileen Severs, a former dental nurse, was much busier. She was a keen member of North Luffenham golf club, she was very active in the Rutland Volunteer Bureau, Age Concern and the Citizens Advice Bureau, and she did voluntary work at Ashwell prison where she taught the inmates to play bridge. She had been awarded an MBE in 1989 for her charity work.

Derek, a regular lunchtime patron of the Finch's Arms pub in the village, had failed to turn up on Sunday 14th November and on subsequent days. Eileen had been missing since the same date, having last been seen in public at an event at Oakham Congregational Hall. The fact that a couple known for their regular habits and reliability were failing to turn up for prearranged appointments meant that the police soon became as alarmed as the neighbours. Derek Severs weighed over 20 stones and had arthritis, which made walking difficult for him, but his Rover car and his wife's VW Golf were both still at their home.

Friends of the missing couple urged the police to investigate 37 year old Roger Severs, a former public schoolboy who had returned to live with his parents in April after breaking up with his girlfriend, then taken a flat on his own in Oakham. Roger had told some neighbours that his parents had gone 'down south' to visit a relative, and told others that his father had suffered a stroke and had gone away to convalesce. They were not inclined to believe him as he had often been known to boast and fantasise, claiming that he was a successful businessman or a doctor while he was in fact unemployed following a series of shortlived jobs as a barman, a crop-sprayer and an ironmonger's assistant.

When the police turned up to interview Roger Severs, they found him sitting by the fire in the lounge of the bungalow. The house was warm and tidy and Roger seemed relaxed and confident, thoroughly 'at home'. In a series of twelve interviews totalling five hours, Severs insisted that his parents had gone away by train to London 'for a break'. Asked to explain why the carpets from the kitchen and bathroom had been recently removed, he said that his father had spilled burning fat in the kitchen and his mother had let the bath overflow. He said that he knew nothing about the bloodstains found by forensic scientists in the bathroom. The police did not believe Roger Severs and he was arrested, charged with the murder of both his parents on a day between 12th and 19th November.

Meanwhile, the search for the bodies of Derek and Eileen Severs went on. The paddock and garden of the bungalow were dug up, but nothing was found. Special sonar equipment capable of detecting underwater objects as small as 30 inches in diameter was borrowed from the neighbouring water authority in order to search Rutland Water, a man-made lake with a 24 mile perimeter. Police divers were brought in and a helicopter was also used to search the lake and surrounding areas, including a landfill site near North Luffenham.

The breakthrough came when Dr Tony Brown, a geography and archaeology lecturer from Leicester University, was called in to examine soil samples found under the wheel arches of the Rover belonging to Derek Severs. He found that the plant and pollen particles in the soil could only have come from certain woodland areas in the vicinity. The police were now able to concentrate their searches in these woodlands, and on 1st December the two bodies were discovered in a shallow grave in Armley Woods. Soil on top of the bodies was later found to have come from the paddock of the Severs' bungalow.

Roger Severs. (Raymonds Press Agency, Derby)

Consultant pathologist, Dr Clive Bouch, inspected the bodies at the site in Armley Woods and noted that a blanket had been tied around Derek Severs and fastened with string and two belts. Eileen Severs had a jumper pulled over her head. The pockets of both victims had been turned out. At the later post-mortem examination, he found that the cause of death in both cases was severe head injuries inflicted with a blunt instrument like a hammer or a mallet. He stated that considerable force had been used to smash the skulls, but that Eileen Severs had not died immediately. Neither victim had been able to defend themselves, and the first blows may have been struck from behind.

Detective Sergeant Tom Robertson visited Roger Severs on remand in prison to tell him that his parents' bodies had been found. He recalls that Roger did not respond to the news in any way. 'He just took the information on board and walked away.'

The trial of Roger Severs took place in November/December 1994 before Mr Justice Laws. The prosecuting counsel, Mr John Goldring QC, told the jury that Derek and Eileen Severs were decent, hardworking people who enjoyed their retirement in an idyllic setting overlooking Rutland Water. In contrast, their son Roger Severs had had a series of relationships that failed, and no proper job. He was 'perennially short of money and a habitual liar', frequently asking his parents for money to set up some business venture or other. The year before, they had threatened not to help him any further financially when he returned home after the break-up of a relationship with Mrs Jain Galliford, the mother of his two year old son Tom. Having Roger living at the bungalow did not work, and his father rented a flat for him in Oakham.

Roger Severs resented not being allowed to live in his parents' home and he frequently complained that his mother preferred to help others rather than him. Derek Severs had repeatedly refused to give Roger money to buy a pub, so that he and Jain could start a new life together. When he discovered that his father had lent £10,000 to a bankrupt friend to open a pub, he was outraged. Severs spent most days drinking in local pubs. On 13th November 1993 he went to his parents' bungalow and attacked his mother in the bathroom. The blows were so hard that he fractured her skull. There were no signs that she tried to defend herself, and many blows were struck as she lay on the floor. There was a great deal of blood. It was estimated that it took

Mrs Severs 30 minutes to die, but her son did nothing to help her during this period. While she lay dying, Severs waited for his father to drive home from a lunchtime drink at the village pub. As Mr Severs got out of his car his son struck him at least ten times on the head with a hammer.

Severs wrapped his mother in a blanket, dragged her through the bungalow to the garage and put her into the boot of Mr Severs' Rover. He bound up his father with belts and string and manhandled him onto the back seat. He drove to a wood several miles away where he buried the couple in a shallow grave, scattering leaves across the top to make it look natural. He then returned to the bungalow and coolly delivered a raffle prize, telling people a number of stories to explain his parents' absence. After this, he lit numerous bonfires, burning clothing belonging to his parents, and dumped a bloodstained carpet at a nearby tip. He even enlisted the unwitting help of the couple's gardener, David Earp, and Mrs Galliford's 13 year old son Michael. When the police discovered the couple were missing, Severs told lie upon lie to detectives claiming his parents had gone away for a short trip. But police later discovered a list of 14 tasks he had jotted down that would enable him to conceal his crime. Although he had had the foresight to list the destruction of the carpets, cleaning the cars, and even delivering a raffle prize that his mother had been due to take out, he made the amazingly foolish error of failing to destroy the list!

David Earp gave evidence that Roger had collected him from his home in Oakham on Monday 15th November 1993, in the VW Golf, which had dirty wheeltrims and tyres. He drove him to the bungalow at Upper Hambleton, telling him that his parents were away for four days, though David noticed that Mr Severs' Rover was in the double garage. The gardener said that he saw Roger Severs cleaning the garage floor with Jeyes fluid. Later, Roger put a carpet and some grass cuttings into a black binliner which they took to a dump near Cottesmore.

Douglas Clements, a neighbour of the Severs family, said that on the Monday night he heard a car going to and from the bungalow many times. On one occasion when he heard the car, he looked at the clock and saw that it was 3 am. The prosecution alleged that what he had heard was in fact Roger Severs taking two and a half tons of soil from the bungalow paddock to dump

Derek and Eileen Severs pictured at Buckingham Palace prior to the award of Eileen's MBE. (Leicester Mercury)

on top of the shallow grave in Armley Woods where he had buried his parents.

Other witnesses told the court that although Derek and Eileen Severs led separate lives, they were united in their concern for their son, a penniless misfit who used to claim that his parents would rather help strangers than him. Alan Freeman, a former landlord of the Finch's Arms at Upper Hambleton, gave evidence that Derek Severs had loaned him £10,000 to set up business at another pub, the Noel Arms in Langham. He added that Roger Severs had been very angry and resentful when he found out, and had warned that there would be 'big trouble' over the loan.

Jain Galliford told the court that she had originally met Roger through the personal column of a local newspaper, and that they had become lovers. At first Roger had said that he was a gynaecologist, but later he had claimed to be an agricultural salesman. In October 1990, Roger had moved in with her to help run her

A 14-point checklist of 'things to do' prepared by Severs to cover up his crimes.

hotel in Lutterworth, and a year later they had a son, Tom. By April 1993, she had had enough of Roger's lies and deceit and had thrown him out. Mrs Galliford told the court that she was totally dominated by Roger Severs, who 'needed to be powerful at all times'. She said that on the day of the killing she had a row with Roger on the telephone. On Tuesday 16th November, three days later, Roger had sent her roses, declaring his love for her. The following day he turned up and took Jain for a romantic dinner. He told her that his parents were away, but that he had sorted out his longstanding difficulties with them. When he paid for the meal he took out a roll of banknotes, and spoke about marrying Jain and buying a pub of their own. Jain described Roger Severs as very intelligent, but too lazy to hold down a job. His attitude to work and his 'total dominance' were the main reasons why they had split up.

Michael Galliford, Jain's son from a previous marriage, said that five days after the killings he helped Severs clean out the cars with a vacuum cleaner, the debris being put into bags and taken to a dump. He also reported how he had inadvertently helped to burn on a bonfire things Roger had wanted destroyed. When he had asked why they were burning Derek Severs' property, Roger had replied, 'Grandad won't need them any more.'

Dr Clive Bouch, the consultant pathologist, described how considerable force had been used to smash the skulls of Roger Severs' parents with a hammer-like instrument. He said that Mrs Severs had been struck about eight times and Mr Severs ten.

When Roger Severs took the stand he admitted killing his parents, but claimed that it was manslaughter due to diminished responsibility. He said that he had been using a steak mallet while preparing meat for tea. He followed his mother into the bathroom where she made some comments to him. He had struck his mother with the mallet. Roger then ran outside followed by his father, who had been in another part of the bungalow. He then struck Derek Severs with the mallet. He could not remember how many times he had struck his parents. 'I have hardly any recollection of what happened,' he said. 'It was a cold night and the cold seemed to start slowly bringing my senses round a bit. I recall that I had a whisky bottle and I drank a substantial quantity. I did not realise what I had hit my father with, or how many times. I sat by the greenhouse for quite some time. The lights of the bungalow were on. I thought about what had happened and went inside. I just could not believe the events. At some stage I passed out.'

Severs told the court that he had been at the bungalow to discuss a possible reconciliation with Jain Galliford. He spoke about it with his mother but the discussion got nowhere. When his father returned from the Finch's Arms, he made a critical remark about Mrs Galliford. 'His comments were not very pleasant about Jain or myself,' Severs added. Under cross-examination by the prosecution, Roger Severs agreed that he had been an accomplished liar and a confidence trickster for a number of years. He said that his mother had once described him as a pathological liar. He also admitted that before the discovery of his parents' bodies he had lied considerably to the police, maintaining that his parents were still alive. He explained that he had hoped this would gain him some time to spend with his son, but that he had been arrested earlier than he anticipated.

Severs told the court that in the days leading up to the killings he had been in a confused, emotional and tearful state because his plans for a reconciliation with Jain Galliford were not progressing. He had been drinking excessively. The prosecuting counsel suggested that Severs had made up the story about preparing steak as an excuse for being armed with the mallet, pointing out that Severs had told the police that he and his parents were having lamb chops that day. He also suggested that Severs' only hope of a reconciliation with Jain Galliford was if he could obtain enough money for them to set up a business together. Severs agreed that he had no job, no money, and that he had hoped for a loan from his father to start a new life with Jain. He also admitted that after the death of his parents, but before taking their bodies to Armley Woods, he had searched the bungalow to see if they had left a will because he wanted to see who would benefit.

A psychiatrist called by the defence claimed that Severs was clinically depressed at the time of the killing and that his responsibility was substantially affected. Dr Peter Wood, a consultant psychiatrist called by the prosecution, disputed this, saying that in his opinion there was no evidence that he was suffering from depression. 'Following the events,' he pointed out, 'there was clearly a high level of activity in a complicated and an organised way to cover up what happened, extending beyond the practical thing of disposing of his parents' bodies.' Dr Wood described Severs as having a basic make-up which made him different from the ordinary man in the street. 'He is a Walter Mitty type of character. The evidence I have seen and heard suggests he is a callous, detached individual who lies and cheats and can be aggressive. He is unreliable, untrustworthy, boastful and grandiose, claiming attributes he does not have.'

The jury of six men and six women took less than two hours to bring in a verdict that Roger Severs was guilty of murdering his parents. The judge told the defendant, 'There is only one sentence and that is life imprisonment.' After the trial, DS Tom Robertson, whose investigative work had been commended by the judge, said, 'Severs is evil and I am extremely pleased with the result.' John Kavanagh, a retired Detective Superintendent, said it was clear that a number of people had been duped and deceived by Severs, who used all sorts of guises. 'Few people knew the real person,' he suggested.

Jain Galliford, the mother of Roger Severs' young son, said that she now believed that she would have been Roger's third murder victim. In a tribute to Eileen Severs, Jain said, 'She was the best thing that ever happened in my life. She was a lovely and a wonderful lady and I miss her terribly. I am glad it is all over. Justice has been done.'

14

BIZARRE MURDERS AND STRANGE MOTIVES

Most of the murders in this book came about through the common motives of lust, greed, revenge and jealousy. However, Leicestershire does have its share of more eccentric motives. In June 1979, an 88 year old man in the village of Hathern took a shotgun and killed his 38 year old neighbour after a long running dispute about their boundary fence.

After a Leicester wedding reception in July 1973, one guest was stabbed to death by two others after an inter-family row broke out concerning the carnation one of the men was wearing in his button-hole. Apparently, he had promised the flower to someone, then forgotten and given it to someone else.

When a 72 year old woman from Clarendon Park planned that she and her husband should move house in 1986, she ignored her 75 year old husband's extreme reluctance to leave the home they had shared for 51 years. Although they had only moved a quarter of a mile from their old house, he became so distraught that he killed his wife after only five days in their new home.

In 1985, the 22 year old assistant manager in a Leicester shoe shop was stabbed to death by a dissatisfied customer – an American ex-serviceman – in a disagreement over a refund. In 1966, two cleaners at Ramon Knitting Company, in Victoria Road East, were killed by an employee at the factory who mistakenly believed that something they had said had caused him to get the sack the day before.

Two business men were shot dead in 1990 over who had the rights to organise the selling of hot dogs on the streets of Leicester, in a crime wave reminiscent of the famous ice cream wars in Glasgow. Inevitably, the Leicester dispute became known as the Hot Dog Wars. A television film called *The Hot Dog Wars* and based on the Leicester case was shown on Central TV in January 1995.

Sometimes, the method of death can be bizarre, too. Police called to a killing on the Eyres Monsell estate in 1987 found that a man had drowned his common-law wife in a plastic dustbin of home brewed lager, which stood in the corner of the living room.

Even when the motive for murder is the all-too-common one of robbery, life can be held incredibly cheap. In 1982, a young Oadby man was clubbed to death in the course of the theft of £31. Two years earlier, Musejc Mohmed Dhorat, a Leicester car park attendant, was battered to death while at work and £12 was stolen.

Although these murders are strange and bizarre, none of them are in the least humorous. A murder over a trivial dispute is as tragic as one where the motive seems more important or more easily comprehended. To batter a man to death for £12 is as unjustifiable as to kill someone during a million pound bank raid. In the words of John Donne, 'No man is an island, entire of itself; every man is a piece of the Continent, a part of the main. Any man's death diminishes me.' Every murder leaves grieving families in its wake; families who have had a member deliberately taken away from them; families with whom we all empathise. Murder also leaves another family torn apart; the killer's own family is frequently left struggling to understand how they can have produced a murderer.

BIBLIOGRAPHY

Andrews, William *Bygone Leicestershire* (1892)
Crane, Arthur *The Kirkland Papers* (1990)
East, C Wendy *The Green Bicycle Murder* (1993)
Lane, Brian (ed.) *The Murder Club Guide to the Midlands* (1988)
Leicestershire Constabulary 1839–1989 (1989)
Mackintosh, A W P *The Green Bicycle Mystery* (1982)
Palmer, Roy *The Folklore of Leicestershire and Rutland* (1985)
Tanner, Michael *Crime and Murder in Victorian Leicestershire* (1981)
Wambaugh, Joseph *The Blooding* (1989)
Williams, Judy *The Modern Sherlock Holmes: Introduction to Forensic Science Today* (1991)
Wilson, Colin *Written in Blood: A History of Forensic Detection* (1989)
Wilson, Colin & Pitman, Patricia *Encyclopaedia of Murder* (1984)

Index

INDEX

Enderby 76 seq
Etherington, Gordon 85
Evington 32

Farrar, David QC 105–106
Ferrers, Earl Laurence 11–22
Fowler, E G B 54
Fox Wilkins, Dr Violet 55

Galloway, PC James 69–70
Gaughan, PC Joe 69
Goldberg, Jonathan 111
Goldring, John QC 117
Goodson, Chief Constable
Alan 10, 70–71, 73
Goodyer, Chief Constable
Frederick 9, 28
Graying, Dr A B 60
Grimston, Captain R V S 10

Hall, PC Alfred 33–34, 47
Hardy, PC 30
Hathern 124
Hayward, Detective
Superintendent 54
Heal, Moses 64–67
Healey, Sergeant 40
Henderson, C L KC 59
Henley, Lord 18, 20
Henson, Joan 54–60
Hewitt, Sir Gordon 45, 46, 49
Hinckley 9
Hirst, Chief Constable
Michael 10
Holmes, Judge Sir Thomas
Edward 10, 37
Horridge, Judge Sir Thomas
Gardner 45
Hot Dog Wars, the 124
House of Lords 17, 18, 20

Ishaq, Mohammed 97–98
Janner, Greville MP 94
Jeffreys, Alec 80, 84, 91
Johnson, John 11–22
Joiner, Sergeant William 55
Joslin, Chief Superintendent
Peter 70
Judge, Ivor QC 97

Kashmir Liberation Army 93
seq
Kavanagh, Detective
Superintendent John 123
Kirkland, Dr 14–17, 18

Lane, Mr Justice Geoffrey 65
Laws, Mr Justice 117
Leicester 9–10, 23, 25–28, 32
seq, 54–60, 61–63, 68 seq, 94
seq, 99–109, 110 seq, 124,
125
Leicester county gaol 17, 29,
30, 60
Leicester Crown Court 91
Leicester Journal, the 31
Leicester Mercury, the 48, 54,
79, 83, 85
Leicester Royal Infirmary 54,
55, 71, 110
Light, Ronald 32–53
Little Stretton 33 seq
Littlethorpe 78 seq
Loughborough 9
Lount 13, 14, 15, 17
Luddites 23
Lynch-Blosse, Major C E 10

McCullough, Mr Justice 111
McGrory, Superintendent
William 70

128

INDEX

Maddocks, Henry KC 49, 50
Mann, Dr James Stewart 57
Mann, Lynda 76–91, 103
Market Harborough 9
Marshall Hall, Sir Edward 46–51, 53
Mason, DS Mick 24–25
Massey, John 24–25
May, Mr Justice 74
Melton Mowbray 9, 28–29
Mental Health Act 1983 111, 113
Metropolitan Police 9
Mhatre, Ravindra 92–98
Mirza, Janghir 96–98
Mocatta, Mr Justice 63
Mugford, Dr Roger 100
Murphy, John 62–63

Narborough 76–91
National Prison Museum 28
Nikoloff, Sabi 68–75
Nixon, Andrew 65–67
Noble, Dr Peter 74

Oadby 125
Oakley, Gerald 69, 71, 73, 75
Orme, Assistant Chief Constable John 70–71
Osborne, Caroline 99–109
Ottey, Detective Inspector Alan 94
Otton, Mr Justice 91
Owen, Detective Superintendent Chris 65

Paas, John 26
Parker, Michael QC 74
Pearce, Detective Insepctor Derek 78

Pitchfork, Colin 87–91
Pollard, Assistant Chief Constable Brian 95
Povey, Chief Constable Keith 10
Pratt, Sir Charles 18
Proudman, PC John 69, 70, 75
Pugh, Dr Victor 71, 93
Pulka, August 61–63

Raja, Abdul 96–98
Riaz, Mohammed 96–98
Robertson, Detective Sergeant Tom 117, 122
Rudman, Susan and Jim 110–113

Sapcote 92–98
Satchwell, James 29–31
Scalford, Derek and Eileen 114–123
Severs, Roger 114–123
Shenton, Winifred 68, 73
Smith, Anthony QC 107
Smout, David QC 73–74
Somerby 32
Stagg, Detective Superintendent Alan 100
Stalker, John 53
Staunton Harold 11–22
Stoughton 32
Swift, John 29–31

Taylor, Chief Constable John 10
Taylor, Superintendent Bert 41–43, 46
Thomas, Detective Inspector Michael 89
Thomas, John 69, 75

129